SEEING

People

THROUGH

Unleash Your Leadership Potential with
the Process Communication Model®

NATE REGIER, PhD

BK
Berrett–Koehler Publishers. Inc.

Berrett-Koehler Publishers, Inc.
1333 Broadway, Suite 1000,
Oakland, CA 94612–1921
Tel: (510) 817–2277   Fax: (510) 817–2278   www.bkconnection.com

Ordering Information
Quantity sales. Special discounts are available on quantity purchases by corporations, associations, and others. For details, contact the "Special Sales Department" at the Berrett-Koehler address above.
Individual sales. Berrett-Koehler publications are available through most bookstores. They can also be ordered directly from Berrett-Koehler: Tel: (800) 929–2929; Fax: (802) 864–7626; www.bkconnection.com.
Orders for college textbook / course adoption use. Please contact Berrett-Koehler: Tel: (800) 929–2929; Fax: (802) 864–7626.
Distributed to the U.S. trade and internationally by Penguin Random House Publisher Services.

Berrett-Koehler and the BK logo are registered trademarks of Berrett-Koehler Publishers, Inc.

Printed in the United States of America

Berrett-Koehler books are printed on long-lasting acid-free paper. When it is available, we choose paper that has been manufactured by environmentally responsible processes. These may include using trees grown in sustainable forests, incorporating recycled paper, minimizing chlorine in bleaching, or recycling the energy produced at the paper mill.

Library of Congress Cataloging-in-Publication Data

Names: Regier, Nate, author.
Title: Seeing people through : unleash your leadership potential with the process communication model / Nate Regier, PhD.
Description: First edition. | Oakland, CA : Berrett-Koehler Publishers, [2020] | Includes bibliographical references and index.
Identifiers: LCCN 2020002558 | ISBN 9781523086566 (paperback ; alk. paper) | ISBN 9781523086573 (pdf) | ISBN 9781523086580 (epub)
Subjects: LCSH: Communication in management. | Communication in organizations. | Business communication. | Interpersonal communication.
Classification: LCC HD30.3 .R454 2020 | DDC 658.4/5—dc23
LC record available at https://lccn.loc.gov/2020002558

First Edition

26   25   24   23   22   21   20   10 9 8 7 6 5 4 3 2

Cover Designer: Jimmy Chan

I am so proud to dedicate this book to Jamie Remsberg. Our team is blessed to be on this journey with you. You embody the message and purpose of this book.

Contents

Foreword
by Dr. Taibi Kahler

A NOTE FROM THE ORIGINATOR

I just returned from visiting the man I admire most, Dr. Terry Mc-
Guire, former Lead Psychiatrist for Manned Space Flight at NASA
(1957–1994). His supportive and courageous wife Toni recently
passed away from a nine-year battle with cancer, and it was important that he and I spend time together. He had always been there
for me.

At ninety-one, Terry's mind is marvelously active as ever, reading two to three books a week ranging in topics from the latest
research in neuroscience, to trivia and humor. He is the most remarkable person I have ever known and at the same time the hum-
blest. It was more than ten years after we met that I found out Terry
had invented the first high-altitude space suit and the external heart
defibrillator, both while at NASA.

As I was taking in the many pieces of NASA memorabilia in the
room—his awards, autographed pictures from astronauts, models
of jets and shuttles—Terry remarked, "I owe a lot to you."

Quizzically, I turned my gaze to him. He continued, "I want to
thank you again. The heads of NASA thought I was a magical
prophet when I was accurate in predicting that of the five flight mis-
sions where there was conflict, I had advised them of the possibility,
including which astronauts would be involved as well as the dynamics of their conflict. I did it using your Process Communication
Model." I felt honored, and thanked him for all he has done at

NASA—inventions, interactions with the astronauts and their families, contributions to the entire program.

We spoke of many things in those two days—Toni, lessons of life, altruism, honor, and the value of humor. Terry creates several "cartoons" daily, often with witty and poignant aphorisms. Always with a keen insight into human behavior, his observations are well-thought through, as is the case with most highly intelligent people who are also wise.

"Taibi, the business of people is communication. That's why everybody needs to know PCM." I repeated that in my head: "the business of people is communication." Hmmm. Business: the trade we are in; that in which a person is principally and seriously concerned; being rightfully concerned about as a service. . . .

I immediately thought of my view of business just as a profession, but Terry was being Terry, speaking in a metaphor. And he was not only effective, but correct. Profoundly correct.

I reflected on the interesting and serendipitous data that we received from our PCM management seminar participants. In addition to scores of 9.4 on a scale of 10 in value to them professionally, 50 percent of all of these "business" people in those seminars commented at the end in written evaluations how important the information was to them personally—what a difference it could have made and will make in their lives with children and spouses.

I began to think metaphorically: "PCM is the science of communication. PCM is the GPS of relationships. PCM is the MRI of personality structure." I was in a Terry loop, gleeful of the fabric of life that PCM describes.

PCM is the science of communication. PCM is the GPS of relationships. PCM is the MRI of personality structure.

My friend and colleague Dr. Nate Regier describes such PCM fabric in this easy-to-read book, taking us into the intimately personal and business professional lives of the characters. His narrative style invites us into the minds, hearts, and actions of the individuals, allowing us to identify behavior in ourselves and in others. As the characters learn to apply PCM in their daily lives, we realize the value of how to talk and interact more effectively with others in our own lives. And with the turn of each page, have more insight into ourselves. Thanks, Nate!

Introduction

GROUNDHOG DAY

Early in her career as a corporate trainer, Jamie Remsberg, one of my cofounders at Next Element, was in Minnesota delivering back-to-back leadership trainings for a school system. She was training the Process Communication Model® (PCM), a behavioral communication model that teaches people how to assess, connect, motivate, and resolve conflict with different personality types. She delivered the same curriculum over and over for multiple groups within the school system. She said it was like Groundhog Day. By the end of the first week, Jamie was exhausted.

Two things about PCM make it difficult to train well. First, it focuses more on how people communicate than what they say, so the behavior of the trainer is being scrutinized all the time. Second, PCM engages learners at a deep level and can bring up a lot of emotion and resistance as people learn about themselves in new ways and recognize increased responsibility for how they communicate. It's hard work for all involved.

PCM is a model for adaptive communication. It is unique in that it teaches people how to recognize and respond effectively to personality-based communication styles simply by observing behavior. A PCM trainer is expected to use these strategies in real time, especially while teaching the material and interacting with learners. This magnifies a dynamic that all trainers experience: that vulnerable moment when your students know enough to assess whether you are walking the talk.

Anticipating another full week of Groundhog Days with the educators in Minnesota, Jamie wasn't sure where she'd find the energy. She went out for Chinese food on Friday evening to wind down and plan her strategy for round two.

As usual, a fortune cookie came with the bill. Jamie was stunned when she read her fortune.

> The intention is not to see through people, but rather to see people through.

"That's it!" Jamie exclaimed to herself. Her epiphany was two-fold. "This is why I do what I do and this is why PCM is different from anything else."

WHY ME? WHY US?

Dozens of books and dissertations have been written about PCM. Why another book, and why should I write it?

It all started in 2005 when I was a clinical psychologist specializing in neuropsychological assessment and addictions treatment. My supervisor and mentor, John Simmering, told me about this communication methodology in which he had been trained and asked if I'd be interested in taking an online assessment to get my Process Communication Model Profile (PCM Profile) and going over my results. I'm always curious about these types of things, having been steeped in the science of individual differences, assessment, and behavior measurement. I had studied and taken a bunch of personality assessments and used several of them regularly in my clinical practice.

What I discovered changed my life. The results revealed patterns in my behavior that I had never understood before. It affirmed characteristics in me that had always been labeled as problematic by my family, teachers, and coaches. It described with uncanny accuracy how my personality had stayed the same since I was six years old, but how I had changed within it. It predicted with scary precision the types of positive motivation I need to thrive, and how I sabotage myself when I am not properly motivated. It explained with embarrassing clarity the repeating power struggles and patterns of self-sabotage throughout my life.

I was hooked. I had to have this so that I could get even better at figuring people out! "Not so fast," was John's response. "This isn't about other people. This is about you. It starts with you figuring yourself out and taking care of you first."

Thanks to great mentors and teammates along the way, I've managed to balance applying PCM to myself as much as to others. PCM became an invaluable resource for me in my clinical work, making an immediate positive impact.[1]

From then on, I devoured everything I could learn. I studied with the originator of the model, Dr. Taibi Kahler, and was certified in PCM with specialization in corporate, clinical, and spiritual applications. Within a couple of years, Taibi invited me to become a Master Trainer so I could train other trainers. This step, along with further mentoring from Taibi, proved to be invaluable since at about this same time, I was assuming more leadership responsibilities, including being director of the organizational consulting division where I worked.

I was 12 years into my marriage and had three children. My wife was trained in clinical social work, with specialized experience working with at-risk youth. One evening after work we were reflecting on our lives and she asked me, "When it comes to our marriage and parenting our children, if you had to choose between your PhD in clinical psychology or PCM, which would it be?" I didn't even need to think about it. PCM, hands down.

After cofounding Next Element in 2008 with a team of two other PCM trainers, I was really in my element. Continuously training, practicing, and interacting with leaders on a daily basis revealed new facets of the model. I was honored when Taibi tapped me on the shoulder again to become a Certifying Master Trainer, one of only a few in the world entrusted to certify Master Trainers and maintain the fidelity and evolution of the model following his death. In this capacity, I have had the privilege of traveling around the world coaching other trainers, conducting master classes, and experiencing the worldwide impact of PCM, not to mention receiving precious mentoring from Taibi along the way.

I was asked recently how I maintain my childlike enthusiasm for PCM. Because the model is so deep, so profound, and so multilayered, every day is like an archeological dig. I never know what I will find! Dr. Kahler discovered a code for what makes humans at the same time unique and interconnected. My favorite quote from Taibi is that "PCM is about types *in* people, not types *of* people." I look forward to sharing with you the profound implications of this statement for who we are in relationships and how anyone can unleash their leadership potential with PCM.

HOW IS PCM DIFFERENT?

The fundamental difference between PCM and any other model of individual differences is that, at its core, it is a way of life. It's not what we do to people, it's who we are with people.

PCM is not something we do to people, it's who we are with people.

It's more than a tool to categorize people; it's a methodology for assessing individual differences in communication, in real time, and adapting on the fly.

It's more than a model for appreciating personality diversity; it's a way to honor who people are, how they are built, and invite their unique contribution.

It's more than a framework for reducing prejudice; it's a set of behavioral skills and attitudes to leverage individual differences toward shared goals.

It's more than a lens for understanding how people see things differently; it's a deep journey into self-awareness and self-transformation.

It's more than a set of labels and characteristics; it's a shift in mindset that sees the whole person behind the behavior.

It's more than a predictive assessment; it's a window into a person's past, present, and future revealing unconscious patterns of success and failure.

It's more than an analysis of miscommunication and distress; it's a step-by-step guide for getting back on track.

It's more than a tool for managing people; it's a philosophy of leadership with visible behavioral guideposts for the journey.

It's more than another way to prop up self-esteem by affirming "I'm unique and special." It's a personal responsibility roadmap toward transcending ego while preserving the individual within an interdependent and connected humanity.

In the earlier section, "A Note from the Originator," Taibi referenced NASA's astonishment with how accurate and predictive PCM is. While PCM can help you analyze people and predict behavior with incredible accuracy, that's only the beginning. Anyone who stops there is missing the purpose and invitation of PCM.

PCM is about seeing people through, not seeing through people.

PCM is powerful and effective at transforming how people communicate and relate to one another. Here are a few of my favorite testimonials from clients who have worked with PCM:

"PCM is the doorway to self and the WD40 to effective communication!"[2]

"PCM shows you your past and present. It gives roadmaps for self-care, it shows you why you've had issues in the past,

and what you can do in the future to strengthen communication. PCM is the real-life equivalent of counting cards at a blackjack table."

"PCM goes deeper—much deeper—than 'personality profiles.' There is a rich context here for leaders of all entities to allow for more effective relationships, cultures, and outcomes."

"PCM is an important part of our shift to a culture of Servant Leadership within our organization."

For 40 years, a growing community of PCM trainers and coaches have been teaching people about the model. Nearly one and a half million people have been exposed to it. The list of blue-chip clients who have used it is impressive, including NASA, Coca-Cola, IBM, Microsoft, Audi, Hewlett Packard, Pixar Animation Studios, and former U.S. President Bill Clinton. It is being taught by over 3,800 trainers and coaches in 51 countries and 2 dozen languages worldwide. Several books have been written about PCM.[3] Our company just finished a global research study on PCM in partnership with Indiana State University. The results showed that PCM training is associated with statistically significant and sustained improvements in personal and professional efficacy, and between 60–80 percent improvement in a variety of key leadership behaviors.[4]

PCM works, no question. When it comes to models of individual differences in general, however, we have a big problem.

THE PROBLEM WITH PERSONALITY ASSESSMENTS

If you've been exposed to a personality model, you've probably experienced it like most people. You took an online assessment. A consultant presented your results in a fancy booklet. If you were lucky, you got a couple of hours of debriefing. By the end, you may have even been enthusiastic about the possibilities.

Understanding your personality could help you become aware of your strengths and identify your weaknesses, you hoped. It could help you appreciate differences in other people. It might even be able to guide you in selecting a job that's a good fit.

A couple days or weeks later, once the intrigue wore off, it was business as usual. Your booklet began collecting dust along with the rest of the training manuals on your shelf. By then, your company had probably paid the consultant and he was off to the next organization looking for a magic bullet.

Only it wasn't business as usual. It was worse.

People began labeling everyone they met. The categorizers went around acting as if they could figure everyone else out. After a while, your teammates developed tunnel vision, expecting people to act according to their identified personality type. When they didn't, it may even have led to an argument. Hidden bias against certain personality types oozed out. Several teammates hid behind their personality, developing an entitled attitude, expecting everyone to give them special treatment. It was a fiasco.

Learning about personality differences is virtually worthless unless you also learn how to communicate effectively with them.

I'm not against personality assessments. They have value when used correctly. However, learning about personality differences is virtually worthless unless you also learn how to communicate effectively with them. Learning about your personality becomes an entitlement program unless you use what you know to become a better steward of how you're built. Insight and learning should make you more capable of responding effectively instead of keeping you fixed in your old habits.

Take a moment to reflect on these questions:

- What's the point of knowing something if you can't put it into meaningful practice?

- What good is diversity awareness if you have no ability to leverage that diversity through inclusion?
- Why help people find a good job fit if you can't keep them motivated over the long term?
- Why introduce people to fancy categories and labels when they are often misused as weapons?

Personality models that don't teach communication, cooperation, leadership, and management skills are a waste of energy, money, and time. Leadership development efforts that introduce people to personality diversity without going the distance to teach and hold leaders accountable to new communication behaviors are doing more harm than good. Furthermore, unless new learning leads to greater capacity for safe, productive, trusting, and accountable relationships, what's the point?

When I introduce people to PCM and they learn that it identifies individual differences in personality, the most common question they ask is "How is PCM different from the other personality models we've used?" I usually answer by emphasizing that personality only matters when two or more people are trying to get something done, and what matters most is how we adapt our communication accordingly. I pose these questions:

1. How do your leaders individualize communication to engage each personality type? Can you see it and hear it in their daily interactions?
2. How have your policies, systems, structures, and processes been adapted to enable success with different personality types?
3. How do your performance incentive and evaluation systems motivate the types of personalities you most want in your organization?
4. How does your organizational communication reflect the types of language that reaches all personality types?
5. Regarding your mission, vision, and values statements, which personalities will connect with them?

Unfortunately, most leaders and most organizations don't have an answer for these questions. Many are surprised that personality differences would even apply. Some have considered these questions but didn't know what to do next. Very few have incorporated what they've learned into the DNA of their leadership and organizational life. While their intentions are noble, the models they were using left them empty-handed when it came to the most important driver of success: relationships.

THE SOLUTION

The solution is to make the transition from a categorization system that is largely polarized to one that actually embodies personality—a system that enlightens and empowers leaders to build better relationships. People don't need another behavior checklist, color classification, or list of animals. In this book, I'm turning the problem upside down. Instead of teaching another personality or communication model, I will show how PCM can enlighten and empower leaders in a twenty-first-century connection economy. I will use PCM to shine a fresh light on the biggest relevant leadership issues like authenticity, trust, and influence. My experience and our company's research with PCM over 15 years have revealed additional aspects to leadership that are only recently gaining attention, like agility, curiosity, authenticity, self-care, and openness. More than ever, leaders need paradigms and frameworks for transforming relationships.

There are a growing number of leaders who crave authentic connection and want to cocreate a balanced and meaningful life with their families, friends, peers, subordinates, bosses, and clients. People in every generation are recognizing the desperate need for sustainable and sustaining relationships that create possibility and potential instead of draining energy. In this emerging era, even familiar concepts like authenticity need a face-lift.

Transformation happens within relationships. Communication is the activity of relationships. I believe PCM can significantly transform relationships through better connection and communication.

> Transformation happens within relationships. Communication is the activity of relationships.

THE PURPOSE OF THIS BOOK

Here's what I want to accomplish and why it's important.

1. Show how leadership is all about relationships and communication—with ourselves and with others.
2. Provide a fresh and relevant framework on leadership that is consistent with emerging trends.
3. Show how individual and collective concerns can be reconciled in leadership.
4. Shine a more focused light on the inner life of a leader.
5. Give the global network of PCM trainers and coaches around the world a resource that helps them show PCM in action, in leadership, in real life.
6. Demonstrate the power of PCM as a transformative leadership communication framework far beyond just another personality model.

One of the unique elements of PCM is the precision with which Dr. Kahler defined each unique personality type and its characteristics in order to differentiate one from the other. Because of this, many of the descriptions of those characteristics that are presented in this book use specific terminology that was developed by Dr. Kahler and that appears in his prior works. Where this is the case, I make no claim of authorship to those descriptions or presentations, the copyrights to which are held by Kahler Communications, Inc.

WHO WILL BENEFIT FROM THIS BOOK?

Seasoned Leaders Who Are Always Learning and Teaching

My definition of leadership is the ability to leverage the diversity of individual abilities toward shared goals. If you recognize that leadership is a continuous process of learning, discovery, and refinement, this book will stimulate your thinking, challenge old habits, reveal areas for personal and professional development, and unlock new possibilities for you and your team.

Newly Promoted and Emerging Leaders

There are no shortcuts, but you can fast-track your leadership effectiveness. This book will connect a lot of dots for you. It will also challenge you to look past your generational and institutional wisdom and reach beyond what you learned in school. Many of the answers are already within you.

Mentors, Coaches, and Consultants

This book will be a catalyst for change agents who want something deeper, different, and fresh.

PCM Trainers and Coaches

Thousands of PCM certified trainers and coaches around the world are continually seeking resources to help them connect PCM to their target market in the leadership and talent development arena. Use this book to introduce leaders to PCM, as a follow-up to PCM training, and as a framework for showing the relevance and application of PCM in our daily leadership journeys.

MEET KAYLA

Kayla is 27 years old. She was an only child, born and raised in Dallas, Texas, by a father who was a truck mechanic and a musician on the side, and a mother who worked night shifts doing laundry at a local hospital. Her parents weren't around much so she kept busy with friends and school activities. In high school Kayla was on the debate team and the yearbook committee and played for her high school soccer team for three years; she enjoyed anything that involved people and activity. She attended community college to save money and get her general education courses out of the way before completing a degree in marketing and communications from a regional university.

Kayla has had two jobs since graduating from college, both helpful in developing her skills and experience, but neither were fulfilling. Kayla and her boyfriend, Lucas, who is a construction supervisor, have been dating for just over a year. Lucas doesn't understand why Kayla is so picky about jobs, and certainly has his own opinions about employment and leadership, but he supports her goals.

The story begins with Kayla deciding that she needs a change. She applies and gets hired at ProcessCorp, a company with a very different philosophy of management and leadership than she is used to. We'll follow Kayla as she cycles through skepticism, vulnerability, and curiosity while she learns about herself and the forces that helped form who she is, and what it really means to see people through as a leader. She learns about the power of personality diversity in leadership and how the principles of PCM are embedded in ProcessCorp's culture. She gains a whole new, deeper understanding of how authenticity, honesty, influence, self-deception, trust, agility, and self-fullness are integral to great leadership. She also challenges a lot of preconceived notions about why people act the way they do. She gains insight into what it means to see herself through and learns valuable leadership lessons about seeing others through.

HOW CAN I UNLEASH MY LEADERSHIP POTENTIAL?

Ride Along
For an engaging, informative, and compelling journey, you can ride along with Kayla, observing what she learns and soaking up the parts that apply to you.

Get Personal and Make It Real

Do you want to know your own PCM personality structure? Get your PCM Leadership Profile along with a personalized debrief from a certified PCM trainer or coach. From your profile, you will gain powerful, personality-specific insights to unleash your leadership potential, including your preferred leadership communication style, motivational needs, decision-making style, self-sabotage distress behaviors, and a personal action plan for self-care and leadership success. Use your PCM Leadership Profile to join Kayla in her assignments. Complete your own PCM Leadership Design project using the guide found in the Appendix.

Engage Your Team

If you want to use the book in a course or team discussion, download the Seeing People Through Discussion Guide, which is full of suggestions on how to deepen the learning with each chapter.

Bring PCM to Your Company

PCM is available in many formats, including coaching, introductory courses, team-building applications, and intensive skills training. To bring PCM to your company, contact a PCM certified professional near you.

For all these things, visit www.SeeingPeopleThrough.com.

ONE

Hypocrisy

People of integrity and honesty not only practice what they preach, they are what they preach.

—David A. Bednar

Kayla woke up with a renewed sense of anticipation and energy, something she hadn't experienced for quite some time. Today was the first day at her new job at ProcessCorp. "Maybe I will find that passion again," she hoped.

DREAMS OF MAKING A DIFFERENCE

Kayla's first real job out of school was with a marketing agency at which she'd previously done an internship. The great part of this job was she could live at home, pay down her school loans, and get some relevant experience. The compensation and benefits were good.

Kayla's first job didn't last long, though. After the honeymoon wore off, she became restless. She didn't like the stodgy, old-school attitude around the agency. Most of the clients were well-established companies focused more on promoting their tradition and values than anything new and exciting. Kayla loved the people and made some close friends. Although she learned a lot, the work was boring and impersonal. So, she began looking for something else.

An opening in the marketing department at a big hospital in Houston caught Kayla's eye. Working with a team for a health care organization surely could offer the community and people-focus she craved. She applied for the job and was asked to take a personality assessment. Although she got the job, she never saw the results of her assessment and was never told what it was used for. Kayla quit the marketing agency and joined the hospital. Although her close friends at work were sad to see her go, her boss wasn't so kind. His last words to Kayla were "I hope you will mature and recognize the value of what we provided you."

Moving to Houston and living on her own for the first time was an adjustment. Kayla adapted quickly. She was sociable and friendly, so making friends at work, at the gym, and in her apartment complex came easily. Her new job at the hospital was exciting at first. There were new things to learn, a fun group of people, and a message of healing and hope to share. What could be better?

The discouragement set in as Kayla began to learn about the crazy health care insurance and reimbursement climate, changing regulations, and the cutthroat practices to recruit physicians. Patients were just a means to an end, identified by their insurance carrier and diagnosis. Her boss seemed more focused on compliance mandates handed down from corporate than tending to the team. Meetings were overly structured, impersonal, and seemed to focus only on where people fell short. Morale was low and people worried more about protecting their turf than supporting each other. She was disillusioned with the lack of compassion, especially for a health care organization.

This went on for almost two years. Many times, Kayla thought about quitting but she didn't want to abandon her team and didn't feel confident she could find something she really loved so early in her career. She tried to hold on to the big picture purpose of helping people, but she soon became miserable.

The only thing that helped Kayla through each day was her boyfriend, Lucas. They met at the ribbon cutting for a new hospital addition project. Lucas's father owned the construction company that did the project. Although Lucas seemed rather guarded at first, he demonstrated deep loyalty and commitment. Kayla knew he was a man of his word. Lucas was a rock, someone who was stable and trustworthy. They didn't talk about work much when they were together, which was fine. Mostly they spent time together doing outdoor activities and enjoying the food and culture of the area. They got along well with each other's families, which was a bonus.

THE EMPLOYEE ENGAGEMENT INITIATIVE

The final straw for Kayla was the "employee engagement initiative." One day it was announced at a staff meeting that the hospital was concerned about low patient satisfaction scores that were threatening their accreditation. Corporate decided that one way to address the problem was to increase employee engagement. Engaged employees can lead to happier patients and better compliance, the consultants advised.

One part of the engagement initiative involved everyone completing an online personality test. The explanation they were given was that there's not a one-size-fits-all approach to engagement, so learning about individual personalities was important. A consultant came in to meet with the marketing team and debrief their results. The results categorized everyone into quadrants and colors, each representing certain styles and preferences. Kayla's profile identified her as someone who cares a lot about people, values relationships, and wants to have fun. "Duh," she thought, "I knew that already." The consultant directed everyone to share their results with others on their team, explaining that by learning about personality differences everyone could gain greater appreciation for various styles, get along better, and be more engaged. The meeting lasted two hours and included lunch.

There were a few guarded "ah-has" in the room, as well as a few laughs as teammates recognized tendencies among them that were common knowledge but had never been given a name. And there was the elephant in the room, or perhaps the elephant missing from the room: the boss. Kayla asked the consultant why their boss wasn't part of this debrief, explaining naively, "It seems she should be here so she could also learn how we could all get along better." The consultant revealed that executive and C-level leaders were doing their own thing, and that they would be shown everybody's results.

A month went by and Kayla's boss never mentioned the personality test. She saw no change in her boss's behavior either. She remembered the personality assessment she had completed as part of her employment application and wondered whatever happened with that one. Did her boss ever see it? Did anyone even care?

Meetings were just as painful. Kayla tried to talk about her personality profile results with a few peers, which was mostly okay at first, but faded quickly without support from above. The only time people talked about it was when they labeled others. "She's a High-D, so you better hurry up." "There goes Ms. touchy-feely taking everything too personally again." Or, "Hey, she's an introvert so don't try and talk to her."

WE HAVE A MISSION, BUT WE DON'T LIVE IT

Kayla shared her discouragement with Lucas. "I don't get it. They say they want to improve engagement, but they don't seem to deal with the real issue—how we communicate with each other. I tried to be optimistic with the personality thing, but there was no follow through and now people just use it as another way to avoid responsibility or gain an advantage. My boss doesn't seem to care about me as a person or about developing her people. We're just cogs in a machine that claims to care about people, but it's all about the money. There is no compassion."

Lucas was mildly concerned, but didn't know how to help. He listened and didn't say much.

Kayla continued, "We have a mission, but we don't live it."

That must have been a trigger for Lucas, because he sat straight up. "That's hypocrisy," Lucas exclaimed with unexpected passion in his voice. "I couldn't work for a place that didn't walk the talk. My father's not perfect, but one thing I respect about him is that he models the behaviors that he expects from his employees. They might not like some of his policies, but at least they know he has integrity and they trust him. He's not above the law and they respect that."

Lucas's response validated what Kayla was already feeling. She didn't see how she could work for a company that didn't walk the talk. That was the beginning of the end for her. She disengaged emotionally and began looking for something else. Her search was limited, though, because she wasn't sure there was anything better out there. She became disillusioned and cynical. She went through the motions at work, but her heart wasn't in it. She was angry at her boss, angry at the hospital, angry at corporate, and angry at life. She privately blamed them all for her situation. She didn't tell anyone though, because she didn't see how it would make a difference. She felt trapped. She was miserable and depressed. In 6 months she gained 15 pounds and was angry at herself for that, too, but preferred to blame work stress and the cafeteria food. Lucas was supportive, but didn't really get into the emotional stuff with her. Occasionally he suggested solutions or tried to give Kayla advice, but it didn't help.

THE TEN BEST PLACES TO WORK

Whether by pure coincidence, providence, or divine intervention, something happened that set Kayla on a course that changed her life. It was a Saturday morning and she was at a local coffee shop enjoying a cold brew and leafing through a magazine. An article caught her eye: "The ten best places to work in Texas." She started reading. The article described employers who had the highest employee engagement scores and were doing innovative things to build strong and connected work cultures. "Is this fiction?" Kayla thought. "Do such places really exist?" She read one account after another, stunned to find out that there were places where leaders cared about culture, walked the talk, developed their people, and focused as much on the teamwork atmosphere as the bottom line. By all accounts, these companies were successful as well.

"What would it be like to work for one of these companies?" Kayla imagined. She briefly let herself experience the feeling of being supported, energized, and free to be herself. She kept reading. At the end of the article was a list of human resource contacts for all 10 companies. "What do I have to lose?" She whipped out her tablet and began researching the companies, looking for job openings or at least somewhere to submit an application, trying not to get her hopes up.

When she landed on ProcessCorp's website, her immediate reaction was, "Wow, this is different!" She read, "Most companies say people are their greatest asset, yet it's the people problems that most often get in the way. We understand. We help companies improve the human interactions that drive your business success. Whether it's an assembly line, customer service process, or new product roll out, ProcessCorp will help you prevent miscommunication and drama from sabotaging the outcome while maximizing the unique contribution of each person on your team."

Kayla did a double take. "Did I really just read people-processes, people-interactions, prevent miscommunication and drama?" She quickly found ProcessCorp's mission and vision statement and was just as shocked. They talked about diversity as their greatest asset and that relationships were at the heart of their work. And their purpose statement read, "Our purpose is not to see through people, but to see people through."

"What? Are you kidding me? I want that!" Kayla's heart was pounding, maybe from the second cold brew she was drinking, or maybe from the prospect of working for a company like this. She tried to temper her enthusiasm as she searched for their online job listing and application. Again she was surprised. The website indicated they were hiring, but there were no job titles listed. Instead she read,

> *ProcessCorp is made up of people who are caring, smart, committed, creative, imaginative, and action-oriented. Thank you for your interest in joining our team. To help us determine if there's an opportunity for you to thrive and help us thrive, will you complete this application and submit your resume?*

The application was not what Kayla expected. She was asked to submit her resume, but there were a bunch of other questions about her passions, gifts, failures, goals and dreams, and ideal work environment. To her surprise, these questions were much more difficult to answer than she expected. She knew what she didn't like, but had never really figured out what she wanted instead. She'd never felt like it was okay to do so.

Kayla looked at a few other websites, but didn't submit any more applications. She called Lucas to let him know what she had done. He was curious and asked a few questions, but cautioned her not to get too excited.

A few days later, Kayla got a call from ProcessCorp saying they had reviewed her application. They invited her to come in for an interview. She was beside herself with anticipation and a little anxious. After all, she hadn't been confident about some of the questions in her application and was worried she'd get grilled about it.

It was nothing like she expected. The HR director, Bennett Lavy, was friendly and kind. He smiled a lot, complimented Kayla on her sunglasses, offered her something to drink, and even cracked a joke. Kayla thought it was a bit unusual that Bennett would compliment her in that way, but felt strangely at ease. Nothing felt inappropriate or insincere about it. After clarifying a few basic details, Bennett brought Kayla next door to a common area that looked like a living room with couches, comfortable chairs, and soft lighting. Two others were already sitting down, engaged in lively and friendly conversation.

Bennett introduced Kayla to one of his HR partners and Pauline Harris, the Director of Storytelling and Brand Engagement. Pauline explained that her department was responsible for "telling and helping others tell the ProcessCorp story in the most engaging and compelling way. This is how our team members and clients engage around our brand. It's all about the relationship for us. The better we tell the story, the stronger the relationship."

Kayla still had no idea for what position she was being considered but she didn't care. She felt curious and excited. Bennett continued, "We saw a potential fit between your experience, skills, and interests and the work that Pauline leads in her department. We'd love to get to know you better and give you a chance to experience a little of ProcessCorp."

The next 45 minutes felt like 5 to Kayla. The conversation was friendly, upbeat, and covered a lot of ground. They asked what she liked and didn't like about previous positions, and a little about her marketing and communications expertise. Mostly it just felt like a conversation that covered a lot of topics, some of which didn't even seem relevant to a job interview. Kayla never felt like she was being interrogated or set up, even though she disclosed a lot about herself. At times she didn't have an answer, or worried that what she did say wasn't relevant or valuable, but she never felt judged. How refreshing!

Kayla finally asked her burning question: "So what would I be doing?" Pauline smiled, took a deep breath, and explained, "Your education is in marketing and communications. Your experience is in trying to get people interested in products and services. You seem to really love people and are creative and spontaneous. We barely know each other, but from what I can tell, I bet you're a terrific story-teller. You would be helping build amazing relationships by helping us tell great stories." Without even thinking, Kayla responded, "Sounds good!" Inside she simultaneously felt warm and cautious. Warm because of a sense of belonging, cautious because she didn't trust what she was experiencing. And then she blurted out, again without thinking, "I'm in!"

Everybody laughed together. "I love that you are excited!" replied Pauline. "We are going to do our homework and let you know our decision this week. Thanks again for your interest in ProcessCorp. We've really enjoyed getting to know you."

The next few days seemed like an eternity. When the email from ProcessCorp showed up, Kayla held her breath. The subject line read, "We'd love to have you on our team." She read the email:

We are delighted to offer you a leadership position at Pro-cessCorp with the Storytelling and Brand Engagement team. You will report to Pauline Harris. Don't worry, you won't have any direct reports at first. Like everyone at Pro-cessCorp, you are a leader and we want to help you develop as a leader. Here is some information about compensation and benefits. Will you review and let us know your decision by Friday and when you are available to start?

Before the reality had sunk in Kayla messaged Lucas to share the good news. "I got the job! Scared and happy. Can't wait!"

Kayla replied with her acceptance and within a couple of hours she had another email from ProcessCorp:

Welcome to ProcessCorp, Kayla! November 12 works great to start. Your first day will include the usual paperwork and introductions. Most importantly, though, will be your welcome meeting with Samantha Bryce, our CEO and founding owner. It's really important to Sam that she gets to know each new leader we hire. As you know, culture is very important to us. Sam takes this seriously and wants to be the first one to personally welcome you.

Will you please complete this online questionnaire so we can generate your Process Communication Model (PCM) Profile? It will take about 30–45 minutes to complete. There are no right or wrong answers, only what's a best fit for you. It's okay to take your time and be as candid as possible. The purpose of the profile is to help you and ProcessCorp discover the best ways we can be successful together. We encourage you to find a space where you are comfortable and free from distractions. Sam and Pauline will have your results and explain how we use them at ProcessCorp.

We are here if you have any questions. See you soon!

TWO

Authenticity

True belonging doesn't require you to change who you are; it requires you to be who you are.

—Brené Brown

Leadership is your ability to positively influence yourself and others toward shared goals. This requires a kind of authenticity that very few leaders have discovered or developed. This authenticity requires equal doses of self-fullness and agility.

Leadership is not just about others. It starts and ends with how we lead ourselves. You can't lead others until you can lead yourself. "The true work of leadership is always an inside job," says Bobby Herrera, cofounder and CEO of Populus Group.

This inside job of leadership requires permission and courage to really explore and accept who you are. How does personality relate? PCM conceptualizes personality as being made up six distinct types. Each of the types has associated with it a unique set of characteristics, including preferred communication styles and motivators. While one of the types is strongest in each of us, all humans have all six types within their personality in a particular order, arranged much like the floors of a condominium. Everyone has the same six floors, but the order of the floors might be different. Our overall personality architecture influences how we function best and how we are able to access and energize each of the six types to meet any challenge. So when you look inside you will recognize that everything "out there" is also "in here."

When you look inside you will recognize that everything "out there" is also "in here."

Leadership agility involves learning how to access and energize any floor in order to assess, connect, communicate, motivate, and grow.

Self-fullness is about knowing, appreciating, caring for, and maximizing your unique personality structure and all that goes with it. You can't influence yourself properly without awareness and management of your personality. Many people equate authenticity with "being true to yourself." Being true to yourself from a PCM perspective means you can't rely on just one or two of the six types, or adopt an attitude that your strongest part is the best part. Being true to yourself means honoring all six types within you.

None of the types within us exists in isolation. You can't take them out of context. You can't lift one up or tear one down without affecting the others. This is one mistake many people make when learning about personality. It's so tempting to adopt a label and overemphasize one thing instead of becoming more flexible and responsible. They are all a part of us, and they all influence each other. It's important to recognize the unique energies and characteristics of each type so we can become more self-aware and live more fully and authentically.

Leadership is also about influencing others toward shared goals. Great leaders help everyone become more and do more by realizing the potential in their personality. This requires agility, a leader's ability to adapt communication and motivation strategies to connect with and influence all six types in others. In PCM terms, it's affectionately called "riding your elevator."

The foundation for agility begins by recognizing that personality isn't about types *of* people, but types *in* people. You can't appreciate another person until you can appreciate yourself and see the connection between you. Leveraging personality differences isn't about finding the positives in people who are "different" from you. It's about embracing that diversity within you first, then connecting with others by seeing that part of you in them. PCM teaches leaders how to energize all six types in them so that they can positively influence those same types in others.

When it comes to personality, if you focus first on how someone is different, you are shutting down a part of you and you lose your capacity to connect through empathy. This can lead to "othering," and makes it a lot easier to act on prejudice. When you recognize that the diversity within us means we are all connected, then you can also recognize that prejudice is rooted in labeling and judging a piece of ourselves first. Indictment of self is what leads to rejection of others. So, leaders who want to be inclusive must start by including all those types within themselves.

Agility might seem contrary to authenticity. It's not unusual for people to get nervous about adapting their style or approach for others. It feels foreign and awkward, so it's natural to conclude, "This just isn't me." The problem with this conclusion is that it assumes that I have to be something foreign in order to connect with you. That's not at all true. Since we all have all six types in us, the discomfort comes from accessing those less developed parts in us. Agility means finding those parts within me that match another person's strongest parts and developing them so that I can be more effective.

Consider this definition of authenticity through the lens of PCM.

Authenticity = Self-Fullness + Agility

Leadership does not require us to change into something we aren't. It requires us to grow more fully into ourselves. Authenticity is about discovering, embracing, and developing the full capacity of your personality and using that to help others do the same.

Resource guides at the end of this chapter give an overview of the key features of each Kahler personality type in us.

———————

"Honestly, I don't see the point of another personality test," Kayla declared to Lucas. "The last time I did something like this it totally backfired."

"So far you've liked everything you've seen at ProcessCorp," replied Lucas. "Why not go into it with an open mind? You never know what you'll learn."

Kayla found the online questionnaire to be more difficult than she expected. She was asked to rank various sets of statements according to how well they described her. Some were pretty basic, and others required more reflection. Some questions asked her how she acted when she wasn't in a great space. These were the difficult ones. She didn't like to think about it and wasn't always proud of the not-so-pretty stuff. She had her own closet of skeletons and hoped to God that the PCM Profile wouldn't uncover them. She did her best to be honest, trying not to worry about how someone might interpret her results.

PEOPLE ARE NOT THE PROBLEM

Bennett met Kayla in the lobby at ProcessCorp with the same bright smile and friendly tone she remembered from their first meeting. "First on the agenda is your meeting with our founder and CEO, Samantha Bryce. Sam is really looking forward to meeting you today. Can I get you a cup of coffee or anything else to drink while we head to her office?"

Sam's office wasn't what Kayla expected. It wasn't huge, it wasn't a corner office, and it wasn't that fancy. It had a fair-sized desk with a bookcase behind it, a sitting area with several comfortable-looking chairs and a coffee table, and an open space with a whiteboard on the wall. "Sam will be here shortly," Bennett reassured before he left. "Feel free to look around and make yourself comfortable."

On the bookcase, Kayla noticed quite a few pictures of people who looked like family and friends, a couple of awards, several plaques, and some framed letters. One of the letters was a thank you from a customer; another was from a retired employee expressing gratitude for his experience working at ProcessCorp. One of the plaques was a recognition for 20 years of service. The other one contained what looked like a home-made card signed by a bunch of people. Before Kayla could read it, she heard an enthusiastic voice behind her.

"Good morning, Kayla. I'm Samantha. You can call me Sam. I am so glad you are here." Kayla turned around to greet the CEO. Sam's face was not nearly as expressive as Bennett's but she radiated energy and warmth. Kayla introduced herself.

"I see you are checking out my shrine," Sam said. "I like to surround myself with the relationships that give me energy and remind me about what's most important in life. I look forward to sharing these with you and learning about those same things in your life. How about we sit down and get to know each other?"

After some small talk and general introductions, Sam's face turned serious, but not scary. She leaned forward in her chair and took a deep breath. "As Pauline shared with you, I really value and enjoy welcoming new people to ProcessCorp. I believe that while not everyone has a leadership role or title, everyone is called to lead. Leadership is not a position or role, it's a way of life. And leadership is not just about others. It starts with each of us. It starts and ends with how we lead ourselves.

"ProcessCorp exists to help improve relationships so that people can be happier, more satisfied, and more productive. When I founded this company 21 years ago, I had been working in manufacturing for most of my life. I was well-educated in business strategy and lean process management and had more certifications than I can name. What I noticed was that no matter how great the solution, how efficient the process, or how well structured the standard operating procedures, they relied on people to get it done. People are more complicated and messy than any production line. People have feelings, ideas, motivations, glitches, baggage, passions, and relationships. And it affects how they do their work. No matter how hard I tried, I couldn't engineer out the human element. I saw humans as a distraction, a source of inefficiencies.

"I became cynical toward people. I found myself frequently criticizing my employees, believing they were lazy, stupid, and disorganized. I didn't necessarily say those words, but I was thinking them! I thought I was carrying most of the load and complained about others not doing their fair share. I micromanaged my employees and didn't allow them to figure things out or make mistakes. I wasn't happy and I was making life miserable for everyone around me.

"I'm pretty stubborn. It took a lot of suffering before I finally realized that I couldn't get rid of the people. I actually needed them. I began to think that maybe people aren't the problem. Maybe they are actually the key to success. People are the most significant factor in the success of any system or process. In fact, humans, and our relationships with each other, are both the cause and the solution to our toughest problems. ProcessCorp specializes in understanding, embracing, and leveraging the human operating system as a key to success for all other operating systems."

LEADERSHIP STARTS WITH ME

Kayla's mind was racing. "Oh my God!" she blurted out. "That's so true! I get it. I love relationships and people. They are the most important thing. I can think of so many situations in my past where leaders completely missed the mark and treated us like we were the problem. If they would have just gotten to know us, it would have been different."

"I'm glad that you appreciate the value of relationships. That's one of the reasons we hired you. And, it's not about them. It's not about your past bosses, or the other leaders in your life. Your leadership potential starts inside of you."

Kayla immediately felt embarrassed and self-conscious and sunk into her chair, worried about how Sam would judge her outburst. "Here I go again, wearing my heart on my sleeve, and this is what always happens!" Kayla admonished herself. She wanted to apologize but before she could say anything, Sam continued with a nurturing tone. "Kayla, you are a creative and caring person. We are so glad you are on our team. We are investing in you because we know you can make a big difference. My hunch is that you've not been given the permission to really explore who you are, what makes you tick, and how you function best. That's the most important part of leadership, and I want to support you along that journey. You certainly have my permission. Are you interested?"

Kayla remembered her uncertainty when asked those same types of questions on the application. How did Sam know? She had a brief flashback to experiences growing up where she got the message from her dad that her needs and feelings weren't valid. "Don't feel bad, it's fine." She could hear his voice as if he were in the room. Kayla felt a little less self-conscious after Sam's permission, but still expected a "but" at any minute. You know, the but that comes after someone affirms you, just before they tell you what you did wrong.

Nevertheless, she took a risk. "Yes, I am interested. Where do we start?"

"Terrific. There's no right way to go on a leadership journey. I have discovered, however, that there are signposts, traps, challenges, and tasks along the way. At ProcessCorp we've determined some very important aspects of leadership that we want everyone to understand and practice. They are critical to the integrity of our culture, and ultimately to our business success. It's all tied together. We are all on this journey, at different places along the way.

"I have the results of the questionnaire you completed, and we will take a look at some of them today. Before we do that, however, I'd love to hear about your experience taking the questionnaire. What feelings and reactions did you have?"

"I was skeptical at first," Kayla responded. "I've done two personality tests before and they didn't turn out well. It turned into more of a weapon than anything else."

"I hear you," Sam reassured. "You aren't alone. I do want to clarify something right up front. The questionnaire you took is not a test. There are no right or wrong answers. There is no evaluation or judgment. You are okay no matter what the results say. Framing it as a test really sends a dangerous message, though. I think that's where things can get off to a negative start. When we take a 'test,' we are conditioned to think there are right and wrong answers, that we will be graded, or that we might be compared to others. Let me guess, when you did the other personality profiles, did you and your peers compare results, and do you think anyone felt like maybe they were better or worse than someone else?"

"Totally! I remember even during the debrief from the consultant, we were all trying to see each other's results and comparing scores. I remember feeling really exposed and worried when he said that our results would be shared with our boss who wasn't even in the room."

"I'm sorry that happened, Kayla. That must have been tough. Anything else you want to share about your experience taking the questionnaire?"

"Yeah, I found it more difficult than I expected. Some of the questions were really hard. I didn't like admitting some of the stuff about myself, and at the same time, some of the statements really didn't apply to me."

"Me too!" Sam empathized, "I remember experiencing the same thing. That's okay, and thank you for your honesty. Let me tell you a little bit about what's behind the questionnaire and what you are about to see. The questionnaire is an assessment based on the Process Communication Model, a model of personality that focuses on how people communicate with one another. I'll just call it PCM for short. It was created by a clinical psychologist named Taibi Kahler. If you want to read all about the history of Taibi Kahler and PCM, I'm happy to give you a resource.[1] I'll just give you the highlights.

PEOPLE ARE MORE PREDICTABLE THAN YOU THINK

"Dr. Kahler discovered a subtle pattern of behavior, lasting as short as a few seconds, that indicated a person was leaving his or her 'healthy space' and going into distress, about to show more obvious negative behavior. He discovered that this pattern was highly predictable, sequential, and observable, and that it had very little to do with the content of what people were saying, and everything to do with *how* they were saying it."

"Woah, that's crazy!" Kayla exclaimed. "I get that. Sometimes I get a gut feeling about someone and it's not at all about what they are saying. Sometimes it's the tone or even how they look at me. Are you saying that Dr. Kahler was decoding body language?"

"Yes, and he discovered that there were six distinct patterns. Just six. He saw that one of these six patterns was more common and clearly predominant in each person. Even more amazing, this subtle distress behavior usually came just before the obvious stuff we clearly know is unhealthy, like blaming, manipulating, attacking, or shutting down. Prior to PCM, there was plenty of awareness of these blatant behaviors, but nobody had identified the subtle stuff and unpacked how to observe and code it before more serious behavior erupted. Kahler called these patterns 'miniscripts' because they were subtle and happened so fast, and they were so consistent, like a script was playing out. This is so helpful in leadership because it allows us to recognize and intervene before things get worse. It's been a game changer for us at ProcessCorp."

"So how does this relate to personality or the PCM Profile?" Kayla was curious and confused.

"Dr. Kahler went on to study the positive behaviors that correlated with each of the six miniscripts. What he found was that there was a whole treasure trove of other characteristics in humans that correlated with their distress patterns: character strengths, motivational needs, preferred ways of communicating, preferred physical environments, even emotional blind spots that could trip them up without awareness. This is where personality comes in. You'll learn all about it in the PCM Leadership Course you will be attending this month."

THE HUMAN OPERATING SYSTEM

Sam continued, "Unlike most other personality models based on some researcher's intellectual hypothesis, Dr. Kahler had discovered a human operating system, a code for how personality is actually built. He didn't invent personality differences or impose some theoretical model on top of human behavior; he actually observed, coded, and analyzed what he saw. What was totally genius about Dr. Kahler's discovery is that by looking at process (how we say it) instead of content (what we say), he was able to reveal patterns nobody had seen before.

"As he continued his research, he discovered that human beings have all six types in them. In other words, we can show characteristics of all six types. Each type is like a muscle that we can develop. A muscle can do certain things, has certain limitations, and needs certain conditions to thrive. Muscles can be developed by exercising them in specific ways. And, each one can be damaged by not taking proper care of it, overusing it, or misusing it."

"That's so cool!" Kayla was starting to make connections. "So, even though I might have natural tendencies in one direction, I can still develop others?"

"Absolutely, and this is intimately connected to what we call Leadership Agility, the ability of leaders to tap into the energy of each type and adapt their approach to connect with all six types.

"This is why at ProcessCorp we get a PCM Profile for everyone when they are hired. We want to give each person a thorough understanding of their own personality structure so that they can gain awareness of how they tick, and take great care of who they are. Then, through training and mentoring we help leaders begin to develop their agility so they can bring out the best in everyone else's personality. Would you like to see your PCM Profile?"

"Yes! I can't wait."

The cover of Kayla's results booklet was titled *PCM Key to Leadership*. Sam explained, "There are a lot of different ways your results can be presented. This one is called Key to Leadership because the focus is helping you learn about your personality and what that means for leadership. There are many different ways we teach people about PCM at ProcessCorp. They all include the same results of the PCM questionnaire but present it in different ways depending on what we are trying to accomplish. We use PCM for sales, PCM for customer service, even PCM for teams. Regardless of our roles or tasks, personality is an integral part because it influences so strongly how we communicate and how we stay healthy.

"Let's take a look at how PCM conceptualizes personality." Sam went to the whiteboard and drew a picture of six rectangles stacked on top of each other in decreasing length. Surrounding it were five words: Assess, Connect, Communicate, Motivate, and Grow (see Figure 1).

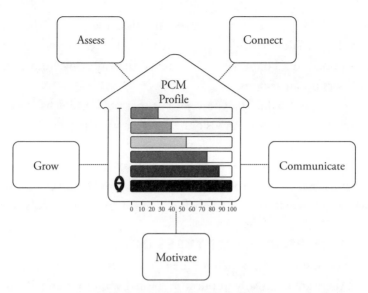

Figure 1. *Leadership Agility: Riding Our Elevator to Positively Influence Ourselves and Others*

Sam explained, "Personality is like a six-floor condominium. Each of the six types is arranged in a preferred, set order. That order can be different for each person. This condo reveals lots of clues about how to assess what's going on with ourselves and others, connect quickly, communicate effectively, motivate for better results, affirm and value people's unique strengths, and grow as leaders. The bottom floor is the one we were born with and is called the Base. It is the most visited floor of our condo and remains our preferred way of making connection with and experiencing the world for our entire lives. It's pretty much what is meant by temperament.

"The order of the floors in your condo represents the relative ease with which you can energize and mobilize the characteristics of that type within you. The higher ones are less developed. If we have to use the characteristics of these less developed floors too often, or need to communicate with someone who is much more comfortable with those floors, it can be stressful. Have you noticed that some people are super easy to communicate with, and with others it's hard work?"

"Of course." Kayla continued, "Some of my best friends must have a similar Base to me because when we are together, I feel so energized. When we talk on the phone, time flies. Then, there are those high-maintenance people. Whenever I interact with them I feel drained. It's a pain. Maybe we are communicating from different floors in our condos."

"Right on, Kayla! The good news is that our condos have an elevator. This means we can visit any floor we want to in order to access or energize the positive features of that part within us. The length of the bars shows how much energy you have, how developed that muscle is. Another way to think of it is how long you can stay there and interact in that way before you get tired and need a rest."

TYPES *IN* PEOPLE, NOT TYPES *OF* PEOPLE

Sam continued, "Kayla, before we get into more details about each type, there are two really important points I want to share. The first one is that PCM is about types *in* people, not types *of* people.

PCM is about types *in* people, not types *of* people.

"This is so important. We all have all six types in us. What makes every human being the same is that we all have the same set of personality types. We are different in how strong each one is and how we use them. No type is more or less okay, more or less smart, more or less worthy."

"What does that mean?" Kayla asked.

"First, it means that we should never label a person based on one type. Nobody is just one thing. They are a wonderful and unique combination of all six types. A soccer player may have chiseled legs, but he's more than a quadricep. Each type contributes to who we are and how we can reach our maximum potential."

"Wow," Kayla reacted, "that's exactly what we did at my last job. We threw around labels like crazy."

"It's human nature to want to predict and simplify, so we gravitate toward labels that make things seem simple. The problem is that it also leads to stereotypes and prejudice. Prejudice is about labeling people, and making judgments about them based on limited information, even discriminating against them because of it."

Kayla connected with the idea of personality discrimination. "I see what you are saying. The last thing my first boss said to me when I left was, 'I hope you can mature and recognize the value of what we provided you.' Sure, I was young and inexperienced, but I wasn't immature, and I was always grateful for the experience. I think he looked down on me because my personality was different from his."

"Personality prejudice is rampant in most organizations and goes mostly unrecognized, or it gets labeled as something else," Sam replied. "We've done a lot of digging here at ProcessCorp to uncover any areas where we might be discriminating based on personality.

"There's a second big takeaway here. It has to do with why we even care about studying personality. Why do we do this in the first place?"

"To increase tolerance for different personalities," Kayla offered.

"That's an awesome goal," Sam affirmed. "And how often do we get the results we are seeking? Unfortunately, instead of more tolerance, we often get more prejudice and labeling. We might appreciate at an intellectual level that different folks require different strokes, but what do we do about it? Appreciating diversity is great, but it's not the end goal. At ProcessCorp, our goal is to leverage diversity. That means we have to understand, appreciate, *and* maximize the potential in our personalities. We want to interact in ways that bring out the best in each of us. Have you noticed that inclusion is a big focus these days?"

"Yeah, I hear about it everywhere. The big thing used to be diversity, and now it's inclusion."

Sam continued, "Inclusion is the next step beyond diversity. Inclusion is more than appreciating or even celebrating a person's unique qualities. Inclusion means to include and leverage those qualities toward the bigger goals of the organization. People don't just want to be tolerated or celebrated. They want to be included. They want to contribute and be part of something. Ideally, their contribution can also maximize those things which make them special and unique, like their personality. This can only happen when we recognize that all six personality types are within each of us. Only when we come to appreciate those types in us, can we appreciate those same types in others and truly include them."

"This sounds kinda spiritual to me," Kayla mused, almost sarcastically. "Are you trying to say we are all connected and that we have to love ourselves before we can love others? That's pretty out there."

"That's exactly what I'm saying, Kayla. You can't lead others until you can lead yourself. You can't truly appreciate the types in others until you appreciate those same types in you. You can't appreciate another person until you can appreciate yourself and see the connection between you. Learning about personality differences isn't about finding the positives in people who are 'different' from you. It's about embracing that diversity within you first, then connecting with others by seeing that part of you in them.

Learning about personality differences isn't about finding the positives in people who are "different" from you. It's about embracing that diversity within you first, then connecting with others by seeing that part of you in them.

"Yes, we are all connected. You don't have to make it some metaphysical connection if that's not your thing. Even if you just keep it really practical, the truth is that when it comes to personality, if you focus first on how someone is different, you are shutting down a part of you and you lose your capacity to connect. Empathy is a big part of leadership. What better way to connect with another person than to tap into the part in us that matches their experience?"

"I'm following you," Kayla inserted.

"Kayla, will you allow me to geek out on some brain science for a minute? Have you heard of mirror neurons? They are a type of neuron in the brain whose purpose is to sense another person's feelings and help us feel them too. They are the biological basis of empathy. I wonder if mirror neurons can detect where another person is in their condo, in other words, where they are 'coming from,' and energize that same part in us. Wouldn't that be interesting!"

AUTHENTICITY CAN BE UNCOMFORTABLE

Kayla felt skepticism welling up inside her. She was excited about what she was learning, and certainly eager to learn about her own personality architecture, but something wasn't sitting right. Maybe it was Lucas's voice in her head preaching about standing up for what you believe in. Maybe it was her mother's voice reassuring her, "Kayla, you don't have to be anything different than who you are. Don't ever change to please others."

Kayla spoke up. "Sam, I get all this and it's cool. But if we are just riding our elevator all the time, aren't we just trying to be something different depending on who we are talking to? That doesn't seem very authentic. Seems like a chameleon. Isn't leadership about being true to yourself?"

"I couldn't agree more, Kayla. Authenticity is crucial to leadership. In fact, that's what today is all about. Since discovering PCM, my understanding of authenticity has changed quite a bit and I'd like to share it with you. I used to think authenticity was about sticking to your guns and living consistently with your values. Turns out, not everyone relates to that definition. Some personality types really don't define themselves by their belief systems. They certainly value and care about things, but not necessarily a set of convictions."

Kayla remembered Lucas's description of his dad, who defined authenticity just like Sam used to. She asked, "Then what does it mean to be true to yourself?"

Sam answered, "Well, it depends on your personality. First, you have to know who you are, what makes you tick, and how you are built to function best. Being true to yourself means honoring that, and what that is may be different for different personality structures.

"It's not unusual for people to get nervous about adapting their style or approach for others. It feels foreign and awkward, so it's natural to conclude, 'This just isn't me.' That's not at all true. Since we all have all six types in us, the discomfort I feel comes from exercising my weak muscles, not compromising my true self. The hard part of leadership is finding those parts within me that match your strongest parts and developing them so that I can be more effective. To say, 'This just isn't me,' is really an attempt to deny that part in me. So instead of being all that I can be, I am shutting down a part of me, restricting my full potential.

"Kayla, connecting with others does not require us to change into something we aren't. It requires us to grow more fully into ourselves. Authenticity, then, is about discovering, embracing, and developing the full capacity of your personality and using that to help others do the same."

"That's a lot to take in, Sam. I'm not sure I fully grasp what you are saying, but I'm willing to keep going. I'm still dying to find out about me!"

AUTHENTIC LEADERSHIP STARTS WITH KNOWING WHO I AM

"Let's look at your PCM Profile," Sam responded. "I'm going to give you an introductory overview of your results, but I'll leave the heavy lifting to our awesome PCM trainer, Sandy, who will be facilitating your course."

Sam went back to the whiteboard. "Kayla, will you share with me the word associated with each floor of your condo, starting at the bottom?"

Kayla shared the details while Sam re-created her PCM Profile on the whiteboard (see Figure 2). "Do you notice the scale along the bottom that goes from 0 to 100? That number represents how strong that type is within you. The bottom floor is your Base and is 100 percent. The other five floors are arranged in decreasing order of preference for you. The length of each bar represents how much energy you have in that part of your personality. If they are muscles, the length represents each muscle's strength and endurance. One of the

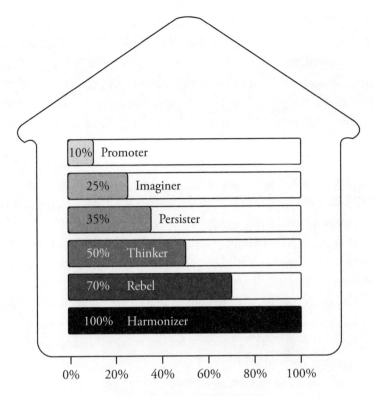

Figure 2. *Kayla's PCM Profile*

cool things about the PCM Profile is that it can measure the relative strength of each type in you.

"See, you have all six types *in* you, just like everyone else in the world. And, you are pretty unique as well. Any idea how many different ways these six floors can be arranged?"

"I have no idea. A lot?" Kayla loved the idea of being unique and connected, but could care less about mathematical calculations.

"Seven hundred and twenty different combinations," continued Sam. "That *is* a lot. The good news is we only need to learn about six types to understand the incredible diversity within us and between us.

"Let's get back to learning about you. The words we have put on the board are the names for each type. Dr. Kahler named them to capture the essential positive qualities that each type brings to the table."

THE SIX KAHLER PERSONALITY TYPES

Sam began, "Harmonizer is your Base type. The Harmonizer in you experiences the world through the perceptual filter of Emotions. This means that you detect and interpret the emotional aspects of what's going on. The Harmonizer type is compassionate, sensitive, and warm. Harmonizers prize family and friendship and want people to get along. That's why they are called Harmonizers. They are happy to spend energy taking care of others, tending to their creature comforts, and helping people feel comfortable."

"Nailed it!" Kayla connected immediately. "That's so me. I've always been about friends and family. I hate it when people aren't getting along. I can sense how people are feeling. My friends joke that I remember everyone's birthdays, anniversaries, and special events. I guess it's because that's what matters to me."

"I'm glad it clicks with you, Kayla. Let's look at the other floors," Sam continued.

"Rebel is next. The Rebel type within you experiences the world through the perceptual filter of Reactions. This means they react reflexively to what's going on, wearing their heart on their sleeve. The Rebel type is spontaneous, creative, and playful. Rebel types prize spontaneity and creativity. They love to have fun and enjoy novelty. They are great at creative problem-solving. Rebels have an amazing ability to live in the moment and change course without getting stuck. They are really flexible."

"Yep, nailed it again!" Kayla reacted, just as her personality profile would predict. She was on the edge of her seat. "I totally see this energy coming out in me when I try new things. I remember that my Rebel part was dying at my first job. Everything was so boring and stodgy. I tried to bring new ideas, but nobody wanted to hear it. Maybe this floor was the one that nudged me to apply to ProcessCorp. I remember something inside me saying, 'Hey, what the heck. Just try it.' Yeah, I was anxious, but also excited for something new."

"I bet so," Sam affirmed. "Next is Thinker. Quite a bit different from the Rebel type. The Thinker type experiences the world through the perceptual filter of Thoughts. This means they analyze and synthesize information, looking for what makes sense logically. The Thinker type in you is logical, responsible, and organized. It prizes data and information. Thinkers want to organize things and find the logical solution. They are really good at planning and completing tasks. They don't mind spending time in their heads working on ideas and plans. Kayla, how do you experience this part of you?"

Kayla thought for a moment before responding, probably energizing her Thinker part in order to conceptualize the pros and cons. "I can see the benefits of this part, and I guess I use my Thinker when I have to get organized and get stuff done, like when I have to fill out forms or complete budgets. Not my favorite thing to do, but I can do it if I have to."

"As we move higher up in our condo, the bars get shorter, meaning we have less energy to mobilize the characteristics of this type." Sam explained, "It doesn't mean we can't do it, but it takes more effort."

"Thinkers are so boring!" Kayla couldn't contain her negative reaction to what she had just learned.

"I'm not surprised you would say that." Sam's eyes sparkled and a big smile erupted. "All that data and analysis all day long! Work, work, work. Crazy, huh? Let's jump in our elevator and ride to the next floor in your condo, the Persister." Sam was exercising her own agility in order to meet Kayla at her Rebel floor with playful reactions.

"The Persister part in you experiences the world through the perceptual filter of Opinions. Opinions are all about making evaluations about how what's happening around us compares to our values and beliefs. The Persister type in us is the judge, comparing the facts of the case against the law and rendering an opinion. The Persister type is conscientious, dedicated, and observant. It cares deeply about doing what's right. Persisters prize loyalty and trust. They want to know they can count on others to follow through on promises and uphold their values. Walking the talk is important to them. They are like the moral rudders on a ship, helping keep things going in the right direction."

"That's Lucas." Kayla was making connections. "This must be my boyfriend's Base type. He is just like this. He's the most dependable, consistent, and loyal person I've ever met. It bothers him when people don't stand up for their beliefs. Hypocrisy drives him crazy! And his dad is just the same. That's probably why he admires his dad."

"I love that you are seeing these qualities in others around you," Sam affirmed. "Appreciating and leveraging others' personality traits is an important part of leadership. How do you see it coming out in you, Kayla?"

Kayla paused. This time it took her a lot longer to answer, most likely because the Persister part in her had only about 35 percent energy. "I'm not sure. I guess it must be important because I respect that about Lucas." She paused again. "I guess you could say that I'm committed to people in my life. I believe that you should always love them unconditionally and be there for them, especially during tough times. Is that my Persister floor talking, or my Harmonizer Base?"

"Great question and great observation, Kayla." Sam explained, "None of our floors exist in isolation. You can't take them out of context. This is one mistake many people make when learning about personality. It's so tempting to adopt a label and overemphasize that one thing instead of becoming more flexible and responsible. They are all a part of us, and they all influence each other. It's important to recognize the unique energies and characteristics of each type so we can become more self-aware and live more fully and authentically.

"At the same time, PCM is just a model. This diagram on the board is just a representation of patterns that Dr. Kahler discovered. It's only a map, not the terrain. Maps help us understand and navigate the terrain, but they aren't the actual thing. The best maps are the ones that best represent the terrain and help us safely reach our destination."

"I get it," Kayla responded, "We aren't just one thing. We are a mix of them all."

"Exactly." Sam continued, "Next is Imaginer with about 25 percent energy. The Imaginer part experiences the world through the perceptual filter of Inactions. This means they take in the world around them in a more contemplative way, experiencing it without a need to analyze, react, or form an opinion. Inaction means the action is on the inside. The Imaginer in you is imaginative, reflective, and calm. Imaginers are quite introverted, yet incredibly receptive to the world around them. If you could see inside their head, you'd be amazed at the wonderful imagination happening in there. They may not be logical and structured like the Thinkers, but they can come up with some pretty brilliant ideas and solutions using their imagination. They prize privacy and their own space. They aren't energized by being around people like some of the other types. How does this sit with you, Kayla?"

"I gotta be honest with you, Sam. I'm struggling with this one. I don't get people who have strong Imaginer in their personality. I never know what's going on inside their head. I don't have anything against them, I just don't understand them. I think my mom had a lot of Imaginer energy. She worked alone at her job and seemed perfectly happy with that."

"I hear you, Kayla. This is the third floor up in my condo. It's a bit more accessible for me, but still it's taken some time for me to really make friends with it and recognize all it has to offer me. No problem. Ready to pull down the ladder and climb into the attic?" By using an active, playful metaphor, Sam continued to appeal to Kayla's strong Rebel floor as a way to help maintain her energy to explore further up in her condo.

"Okay. What am I going to find up there?" Kayla smiled but felt a little apprehensive.

Sam continued, "The Promoter part experiences the world through the perceptual filter of Action. They are always on the go, looking for what to do next. The Promoter in you is adaptable, persuasive, and charming. This part brings the charm and is naturally charismatic. Promoters prize self-sufficiency because they are highly adaptable. Drop them in a strange situation with a paperclip and bottle of water and watch them take advantage of the opportunities. Promoters thrive on risk and excitement. They don't mind competitive environments and love the limelight."

"Ugh. I feel icky." Kayla couldn't contain her discomfort.

"It's okay," Sam assured her.

"Sam, did you notice what I just did?" Kayla had an out-of-body experience as she observed the process of how she was communicating. "I just reacted by saying Ugh! Then I shared a feeling, icky. I can see my strongest personality types in me coming through loud and clear."

"Right on, Kayla," Sam replied. "It's amazing what we can see when we start paying attention to the language of personality."

"So back to the Promoter," Kayla continued. "The Promoter seems so slimy, like a used car salesman trying to take advantage of me. I've known some of these types and I didn't like them. I never felt comfortable around them. So, maybe it's okay not to make friends with that part of me? Is that wrong?"

Sam sensed that Kayla was communicating from her Base Harmonizer because of the shift in focus to feelings and concern for how others feel. So Sam energized her own Harmonizer part in order to respond. "What you are experiencing is totally normal, Kayla." Sam's voice was supportive and affirming. "Often this is how people experience the least developed parts of their personality. It feels foreign, strange, and uncomfortable. You haven't spent much time there, so I can totally appreciate that you aren't familiar with all the positive potential this type brings to your life."

Kayla smiled and seemed to relax. Sam interpreted this as evidence that Kayla had accepted the Harmonizer connection and now had energy to continue.

"There's another side of this we haven't talked about. Distress. Remember the miniscripts? These were distress patterns, the not-so-pretty stuff. Everyone has them, including the Promoter. That slimy stuff you mentioned is typical of Promoters in distress, not how they act when they are in a good space. Maybe you've experienced Promoter distress from these people which makes it difficult to see the positives. You'll learn all about that in your PCM course."

Kayla felt reassured. "I get what you are saying. You know what else I just realized? If Promoter was my Base and I was communicating with my current self, I bet that would be really tough. Promoters prize self-sufficiency and Harmonizers prize connections and togetherness. Those seem really opposite!"

"Way to use your Harmonizer superpower of empathy, Kayla! Now that we've covered all six types in you, I'm curious to hear about your experience. How are you feeling about this? What are your reactions?" Sam appealed to Kayla's two strongest perceptual frames of reference, emotions and reactions, because she knew that people are most comfortable and energized when they can speak with their favorite perceptual language.

"Well, I definitely feel like my profile is accurate. I could feel the energy draining out of me as we went higher and higher in my condo, so it made a lot of sense. Somewhere just after the Thinker floor I noticed I was trying to distance myself from it. It was like I didn't want to admit these next three floors were part of me."

"Anything else?"

"Yeah," Kayla continued, "I kept thinking about other people in my life who have strong Persister, Imaginer, or Promoter energy. I found myself labeling them as if they were that one type. I heard myself saying things like, 'Yep, those Imaginers are so antisocial.' I don't dislike them, and I accept people who are different from me, but I also don't get along with them the best."

"Are you aware that you just labeled someone as Imaginer and called them antisocial?" Sam's voice was serious again.

Kayla looked down at her lap and felt self-conscious again, a highly predictable behavior of Base Harmonizer personality types when experiencing stress. Only this time she understood what was happening. "Wow, just because I am a Harmonizer Base doesn't mean I am free from prejudice. I just now understood what you said earlier about personality discrimination. I labeled, made assumptions, and jumped to a negative conclusion about a personality type that's less developed in me. Everyone talks about unconscious bias these days. Some of my biases come from the top floors of my condo."

"Kayla, that is great insight and hard stuff to recognize. Awesome. You are worthwhile. They are worthwhile, and it's easy to form negative impressions about types in us that are less developed.

"We've covered a lot today and our time is almost up. Thank you for your openness to learn about yourself and consider this new way of looking at who we are as people. The first step in seeing people through is to embrace and appreciate all six types in you.

"It's important to me to personally share the ProcessCorp philosophy with each employee, and to do the introduction to PCM. This is how I get to know each person and convey the value we have for each unique personality structure in our company. You are no exception. You are a very special person with a unique personality that has so much potential. You will learn how to use your personality to stay healthy, motivated, and make the biggest contribution possible. Over time you will also learn how to influence others to do the same. We call it 'seeing people through.' It's a leadership philosophy for life, and PCM can help you along the way."

"Thank you so much, Sam, for taking the time to make this personal connection. I'm pumped to learn more." Kayla was feeling grateful and excited.

"Your meeting with me was the first appointment of your first day at ProcessCorp so I could give you a big welcome aboard. We've covered all six types within each person. We've touched on the perceptual frames of reference and signature character strengths for each one. As you go through your orientation, I encourage you to pay attention to see how these show up in you and in the people you meet."

Kayla immediately felt pressure inside, as if she was going to be evaluated. Sam must have sensed it because she continued with a reassuring tone. "Kayla, there is no expectation that you do anything with this right now. All I'm saying is that with your new 'PCM eyes and ears' you might notice things you didn't realize were important. Enjoy!"

"I can do that, Sam! Thanks for the encouragement."

"Good luck with your orientation, Kayla. I know you have a packed schedule today, and will be meeting regularly with Pauline to continue learning about PCM and seeing people through. Remember, it's okay to trust your gut and have fun. We are so glad you're here!"

Kayla knew she'd made the right decision.

RESOURCE GUIDES

Table 1: The Six Kahler Types, Perceptual Frames of Reference, and Typical Words and Phrases

Personality Type	Perceptual Frame of Reference	Typical Words and Phrases to Look For
Thinker	Thoughts	I think, options, data, time frames, who, what, when, where, facts, information
Persister	Opinions	I believe, in my opinion, we should, respect, values, integrity, admiration, commitment, dedication, trust, virtue
Harmonizer	Emotions	I feel, I am comfortable with, happy, sad, love, care
Rebel	Reactions	I like it, I hate it, I want it, I don't want it, Wow!, sounds like fun
Imaginer	Inactions	I imagine, not sure, wait for more direction, hold back, easy pace, my own space, need time to reflect, don't want to rock the boat
Promoter	Actions	Let's go, make it happen, go for it, the bottom line, do it

Table 2: The Six Kahler Types, Character Strengths, What They Prize, and Hidden Bias

Personality Type	Character Strengths	What They Prize	Hidden Bias
Thinker	Logical, responsible, organized	Data and information	People who don't think clearly
Persister	Conscientious, dedicated, observant	Loyalty and commitment	People who aren't committed
Harmonizer	Compassionate, sensitive, warm	Family and friendship	People who don't care about others
Rebel	Spontaneous, creative, playful	Spontaneity and creativity	People who are boring
Imaginer	Imaginative, reflective, calm	Privacy and their own space	People who want to interact all the time
Promoter	Adaptable, charming, persuasive	Self-sufficiency and adaptability	People who don't take initiative

THREE

Honesty

Old-school business views the expression of emotions and compassion as vulnerability; today's new business people see such attributes as the glue that binds us.
—*Keith Ferrazzi,* Never Eat Alone

Most conflict can be explained by a gap between what we want and what we get. Ken Blanchard, leadership guru and best-selling author, describes it as a gap between what we are experiencing and what we want to be experiencing.

Conflict produces energy which can be experienced physically, possibly manifesting as a racing heart or tension in the neck, or emotionally, such as fear, anxiety, or excitement. Conflict isn't inherently bad, but the energy it produces can be used in destructive ways. In many cases, destructive conflict in relationships starts with failing to be honest about what's going on with ourselves emotionally.

Many leaders practice safe honesty, convincing themselves that they are being authentic and transparent by telling the truth. Safe honesty means telling the factual truth, or sharing your opinion. The reason that it's safe is that in most cases your truth-telling has no impact on your own vulnerability. Telling someone your opinion about them, or letting them know the facts about their performance, only makes them more vulnerable. It's harder on them than it is on you. That's safe honesty.

Real honesty means doing the tough emotional work. It means getting in touch with our own emotional responses to situations, and our emotional motives. If I am feeling anxious and I want to feel secure, then security is my emotional motive.

Whether or not we are aware of them, whether or not we tell people about them, emotional motives are constantly influencing us. Safe honesty avoids talking about these because we have convinced ourselves they aren't important, or we fear rejection. Or, we might simply be unaware.

PCM helps us identify personality-specific emotional motives. Each PCM personality type has an emotional issue associated with it, and that emotional issue is uniquely challenging because the strengths of that type aren't well suited to deal with it; it doesn't sync well with the modus operandi of that type. When life presents us with that issue, it can be challenging. So, getting honest about the issue really stretches us to get vulnerable, ask for help, and lean on the strengths of our other floors in our personality condo. That's real honesty and it requires doing the hard emotional work.

Avoiding real honesty doesn't solve the problem. PCM predicts with uncanny accuracy how blocked or displaced emotional motives morph into self-sabotaging cover-up behavior.

The good news is that, contrary to popular leadership lore, emotional transparency and vulnerability are not weaknesses. They are a sign of courage, authenticity, and emotional intelligence. Doing the hard emotional work forges connections that build trust. Honesty is a key ingredient in seeing ourselves through, and seeing others through.

Resource guides at the end of this chapter summarize the emotional issues and personality dynamics for each personality type, predictable distress behavior when we attempt to cover it up, and affirmations to encourage leaders in doing the hard emotional work.

Kayla's first day at ProcessCorp included meetings with Human Resources, IT, and introductions to the other people in her department. Everyone was kind and welcoming. Kayla had lunch with Pauline, her department head and supervisor. Mostly they talked about how the Storytelling and Brand Engagement department functioned and what kind of work Kayla would be doing. Two things stood out about Pauline. First, Pauline used a lot of feelings and reactions language. Instead of asking Kayla what she thought about things, Pauline would say, "I'd like to hear how you feel about this." And, she used upbeat reactions as well, with language like, "I love that!" or "That's terrific."

At first Kayla wondered if Pauline just happened to have the same personality structure as she did. But the more she listened, the more she began to pick up on a common thread of action verbs. When she was sharing her own perspective, or was excited about something, Pauline would use phrases like, "This is how we do it here," or "I'm gonna cut to the chase." "Maybe Promoter is Pauline's Base type," Kayla hypothesized.

When Kayla met with Bennett, she was quite impressed with his personality agility. He obviously had a strong Harmonizer part in him, because he was always so kind and affirming. He complimented her classy shoes. She realized that he was meeting her where she was at, using language that matched her strongest personality part. He didn't treat everyone with the same warmth, though. With some people he kept things very focused on data and time frames. With others he seemed to be more focused on the relevant principles that applied to the conversation.

Kayla was excited to tell Lucas about her first day, especially her meeting with Sam. She invited Lucas to pick up some takeout and come over after work so she could show him her PCM Profile and tell him about her day. Lucas didn't share Kayla's enthusiasm. "This all seems like a lot of new-age stuff, Kayla. It's all fine and good to learn about personality, but how are they really going to treat you when the novelty wears off. You gotta guard yourself and watch out. Don't get too excited because this is probably too good to be true. Don't get me wrong, I'm happy for you, but in my opinion, it's just part of them trying to put on a good show in the beginning. It won't last."

Kayla felt defensive and deflated. She wanted Lucas to support her and share her enthusiasm, but she also trusted his steady perspective. He never seemed to get too excited about things and could see the big picture. She knew he just wanted to protect her. Still, she felt angry but didn't say anything. She noticed herself getting quiet while they ate dinner. Then, a light bulb went on in her head when she recognized that Lucas was operating from his Persister floor when he shared his opinions and skepticism. "I have that same part in me!" Kayla realized. "I can use it to balance my Rebel enthusiasm with careful observation and listen to my conscience." She didn't know what to do with her realization, but tried something new.

"Lucas, I appreciate your caution. Thanks for sharing your opinion and wanting to make sure I am treated well."

Lucas looked up from his plate with surprise on his face. "That's what I was trying to say, Kayla. I want you to be treated with respect. Pauline seems okay. She's a no-nonsense person. I respect that."

All of a sudden Lucas appeared less critical. Kayla concluded that when she validated his strongest perceptual frame of reference, Opinions, he in turn was more open to her situation. She made a mental note: "If I want Lucas to hear me, I can use my Persister to gain empathy, then I can meet him where he's at by speaking his language."

On Wednesday of her first week Kayla attended the first module of the PCM Leadership Seminar with several other new hires. She learned about the history of PCM and Taibi Kahler, the structure of personality, and all about the demographics of each Kahler personality type. Kayla was fascinated by how accurate the features were, like typical office and home environments. She learned in more detail about the six perceptual frames of reference and signature character strengths of each personality type. The group practiced energizing different floors in their condos and speaking the language of that type. This gave her more confidence to take Sam's invitation to observe behavior around her, and even try matching their personality energy like she had with Lucas.

Part of Kayla's orientation was spending time with Mario, a designer in Pauline's department. She noticed that he used a lot of Thoughts perception language, always asking questions to clarify his understanding of the facts, or talking about data and time frames.

Kayla attempted to match his Thinker energy by going to her Thinker floor and paying attention to what mattered to him. She asked him about the factual details of his job, and complimented his organization and knowledge around his work. He seemed to really appreciate it. Kayla was surprised how quickly rapport could be established simply by validating someone else's perceptions.

CONFLICT? WHAT CONFLICT?

Pauline was in her office when Kayla arrived for their first weekly integration meeting and greeted her with a big smile. "Welcome, Kayla! I'm so glad to see you today. I've been looking forward to our time together." Kayla felt seen and affirmed for who she was.

Pauline started, "Kayla, I bet you are starting to experience the different personality types in you and what's most comfortable for you. I'm curious where you'd like to sit today. I have a lot of options in my office. What feels best?"

Kayla pointed to a comfortable chair she had sat in once before. "Make yourself comfortable and we'll get started," Pauline directed. "What's been on your mind since we last met?"

Kayla shared some of her insights, including her interactions with Lucas and her insights about meeting people where they are at by matching their personality perception. She finished with a comment that popped out unexpectedly: "I was kinda mad at Lucas because he didn't take me seriously. He's such a skeptic."

"I hear ya, Kayla." Pauline affirmed, "It's often tough sharing new stuff with someone else, especially when you are excited about it and they are hearing it secondhand. Ah, the joys of conflict."

"What do you mean, conflict? What conflict? It turned out okay." Kayla felt a little defensive.

Pauline continued, "Maybe things didn't blow up, but certainly there was a gap between what you wanted and what you experienced from Lucas. Am I reading that right?"

"Yeah, that's true. I wanted him to listen to me and validate what was important to me," Kayla admitted.

"Totally! And it seems he was less critical after you validated his Persister frame of reference. But there's still a gap. What a perfect segue for what I'd like to talk about today." Pauline continued, "I'd like to explore with you the role of honesty in leadership and relationships."

"I'm confused," Kayla said. "What does this have to do with honesty? Maybe Lucas could have been a bit less honest with his opinions!"

LEADERSHIP IN THE GAP

"I owe you an explanation, Kayla. Most leadership happens in a gap; it's the gap between what we want and what we are experiencing at any point in time. Maybe I want to feel heard, and you don't listen to me. Maybe I want to feel confident in my new role and I don't know what I'm doing yet. Gaps are everywhere. Within us and between us. Gaps between what we want and what we are experiencing are normal and might be the most basic form of conflict. What's also normal is the energy produced by the gap. I feel that energy when my heart races and I get tension in my neck and shoulders. What about you?"

"I feel it in my stomach and a lump in my throat," Kayla responded. "I can remember even when I was little, I'd get stomachaches when there was conflict. Last week with Lucas I felt a lump in my throat when I shut down at dinner."

"That's great self-awareness, Kayla. Knowing how gap energy shows up for you is so critical in leadership because it's a sign that something is going on that needs to be addressed.

"There's nothing wrong with this type of conflict. Gaps are an inevitable and natural part of being human. Because we are built differently and have different wants and needs, we are going to experience conflict. The real question is, what do we do with that energy? Do we channel it constructively or in self-defeating ways?

"Honesty is the first step in channeling that energy constructively. When we hide the truth, we set in motion a destructive pattern of behaviors that moves us farther away from being able to see people through."

"I'm not following you, Pauline. We can't just go around blurting out the truth all the time. That would be cruel." Kayla remembered her first boss speaking his mind about her immaturity when she quit. "Honesty sucks sometimes."

SAFE HONESTY

Pauline smiled, "I'm not talking about sharing your opinions or telling the factual truth. That's what I call safe honesty. If I tell you that your shoe is untied, that's safe honesty. If I share my opinion about how you should act or dress at work, that's safe honesty. Even if I tell you what I really think about your work performance, that's safe honesty. It's honest because it might be a truthful expression of what I think or believe. But it's safe because it's disconnected from the heart, and it usually ends up with you feeling more exposed, not me. Safe honesty is superficial because it often masks the real issue, and usually avoids personal vulnerability."

Kayla reacted, "What do you mean? What am I hiding if I tell you that your performance sucks? That's just telling it like it is." Kayla chuckled when she heard herself. "I sound like my dad! He used to say this all the time like it was a badge of honor."

"I know, Kayla! I used to say the same thing all the time when I started at ProcessCorp. I'm a no-nonsense person and prefer to cut to the chase. In case you didn't know already, my Base is Promoter." Pauline reached behind her and pulled a small acrylic stand off the shelf displaying her PCM structure (see Figure 3).

"Call it what you want; radical candor, brutal honesty, or telling it like it is. The truth is, this type of honesty rarely leads to better connections and stronger relationships. Sometimes it works in certain situations where trust is really strong, and people have an explicit understanding about intentions. Even then, it can backfire so easily, and I can share lots of examples from my own life. Safe honesty doesn't build real trust; that takes something deeper and more vulnerable.

"PCM shows us that there's another layer of honesty, something even deeper that influences our behavior. Something that predicts how the gap of conflict will show up for each of us and what we need to do in order to channel that energy in a productive

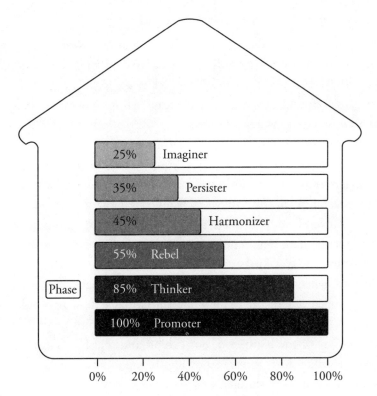

Figure 3. *Pauline's PCM Profile*

way. This deeper layer of honesty cuts to the core of why we do what we do and what our real intentions are. Until we come to grips with this, we are destined to engage in superficial, safe honesty. Would you like to know more, Kayla?"

"Yeah. I agree with you that the type of honesty I'm familiar with rarely feels good." Then Kayla decided to apply what she'd learned in class. She energized the Promoter floor in her condo, mustered her best no-nonsense tone, and said, "Cut to the chase, Pauline. Give me the bottom line on honesty."

Immediately Kayla felt vulnerable, but it didn't last long. Pauline flashed a big smile and replied, "Kayla, that was awesome! You have no idea how perfect that was. Great job matching my favorite perception of Actions. That means a lot."

DOING THE HARD EMOTIONAL WORK

"True honesty is about doing the hard emotional work," Pauline continued. "As humans, our first response to conflict is an emotional one. That's because the gap of conflict is a gap between how we want to feel, and how we are currently feeling. Not many people have enough self-awareness to recognize it. Instead, they cover it up or avoid it until it morphs into something else.

"I'll illustrate with a true story. ProcessCorp was exhibiting at a human resource trade show. I was staffing the booth along with a few others on our team and Sam was scheduled to be at our exhibit booth for a couple of hours to meet several of our clients. Sam had been there for about an hour when I noticed big, dark sweat marks on her gray shirt. She was in the middle of a conversation with one of our biggest clients. I was mortified. I snuck out, ran back to the hotel, and grabbed one of my clean white shirts that I thought would fit Sam. When I got back, I took the first opportunity to pull Sam behind one of the banners of our exhibit and told her, 'Go change into this white shirt. Sweat is showing through like crazy. You know what our clients will think!'

"Sam was stunned. She thanked me for saving her and did as I directed, returning shortly to continue conversations with our clients. She commented later about being stupid for wearing a gray shirt. We didn't talk about that incident for over a year, but it put a wedge in our relationship."

"How so?" Kayla asked. "Sounds like you saved the day. Wasn't Sam grateful?"

"Yes and no. I practiced safe honesty and it nearly ruined our relationship. When I first saw the sweat showing through Sam's shirt, I experienced a gap between what I wanted and what I experienced. I felt embarrassed and worried about what our clients would think. Instead of being honest with Sam about how I felt and enlisting her input around a solution, I just took action to solve the problem and told Sam the safe, factual truth. When I said, 'You know what our clients will think!' I was totally covering up my real feelings by creating negative drama and acting superior to her. I scolded my own boss as a way to avoid feeling close to her and being an ally who cared.

"If I would have been really honest, I would have said, 'Sam, I noticed you are sweating and I'm feeling really embarrassed about how this might come across to our clients. May I go get you another shirt?' But that would have been too vulnerable and intimate for me. Instead, I did just what my personality predicts. I took action to solve her problem without her consent so that I could feel better. That's really self-centered."

"You said this put a wedge in your relationship with Sam. Say more." Kayla was curious.

"A year later, just before we went back to that same expo, Sam finally brought it up with me and explained how she experienced the incident. She told me how embarrassed she was, and grateful that I'd taken action to help. She also expressed her resentment that I wasn't honest with her about how I felt and didn't ask her permission to fix the problem. She wanted to know that I cared about her but instead she felt belittled and small."

Kayla spoke up. "Wow, Pauline, I get it. I can really empathize with Sam."

"Exactly. But Sam didn't say anything about it at the time. She also practiced safe honesty by thanking me for saving her. She was worried that if she expressed her anger it would ruin our relationship and I would think she didn't appreciate me. Instead she acted grateful for the dry shirt and openly criticized herself for making a stupid wardrobe decision in the first place. She held in that anger and resentment for a year and as a result she was hesitant and guarded with me. I didn't understand why and I started to lose respect for her.

"We both practiced safe honesty and avoided the real emotional issues. As a result, our relationship was strained for a year until we got honest with each other."

Kayla noticed her mood had shifted. She felt that same lump in her throat as she recalled how angry she had felt with Lucas when she had kept quiet. She had a rush of memories from her past of times she felt angry but didn't speak up. She recalled just yesterday when Pauline asked her to redo a brochure design and she had felt resentful because nobody told her the specs ahead of time.

After a few moments of silence Kayla spoke up. "Let me see if I'm getting this. Conflict is a gap between how we want to feel and how we are currently feeling. It's emotional, whether we recognize it or not. If we aren't honest about the emotional stuff, we might take action to close the gap in ways that make things worse. Or at least we might solve a superficial problem but create more problems down the road. Am I getting it?"

"Yep." Pauline's tone was warm and empathetic. "Seeing people through includes getting honest about the emotional stuff that's influencing our behavior and interactions with each other."

"How do we know what it is?" Kayla questioned. "I mean, I'm an emotional rollercoaster some days. I have a ton of stuff going on inside. How do I know what I should pay attention to?"

WE ALL HAVE AN EMOTIONAL ACHILLES'S HEEL

"PCM to the rescue!" Pauline reacted playfully. "Remember earlier when I said that PCM gives us clues? Each personality type has an emotional issue that is uniquely challenging and really important. Certain situations can trigger the issue. If we don't acknowledge it and deal with it openly, things can get sideways really fast."

"Do you mean if we aren't honest about it, we might end up going down a path that just causes more problems?" Kayla asked.

"Exactly! You got it. And here's the irony. The emotional issue connected to each personality type is uniquely challenging because the strengths of that type aren't suited to deal with it. It's like an emotional Achilles's heel. So, getting honest about the issue really stretches us to get vulnerable, ask for help, and lean on the strengths of the other floors in our personality condo."

"Tell me the issues." Kayla's curiosity was piqued, and she remembered to use Pauline's preferred perception language of action.

"I will, and first there's one more wrinkle to explain. Throughout our lives we can energize any of our six types in us to experience the perception and use the character strengths of that floor in our condo. And the order of the floors in our condo remains the same. You learned that in your first PCM training module last week. In your next PCM module you will learn about Phase, which is really relevant here. Phase is a designation for one floor in our condo with special significance. One way it is significant is that it correlates with the emotional issue that will be most relevant for us at that time in our lives. So, it's not like people have to deal with all six Phase issues every day. The issue that connects with our current Phase is most relevant.

"You asked about the issues. Let's start with a type that is strongly developed for you and Sam, the Harmonizer. The Harmonizer Phase issue is anger. Why is anger so important for the Harmonizer, and why is it so difficult to be honest about? Because Harmonizers are natural caregivers. Their philosophy is: *It's my duty to show compassion, nurture others, and promote harmony.*

"Because of the nature of humanity, though, people do nasty things, sometimes even on purpose. It's perfectly natural and totally human to feel angry about that. Expressing anger in a healthy, assertive way is really difficult for Harmonizers, though. Their character strengths are compassion, sensitivity, and warmth. None of those help with expressing anger; in fact, it's just the opposite. The Harmonizer Phase person fears that if they express their anger people will reject them, and it will threaten relationships."

"I can relate," Kayla remembered several situations.

Pauline continued, "What if a child with a Harmonizer Phase grows up around people who express anger in passive aggressive or aggressive ways? For a child, the message is that anger hurts people. So it's a natural coping mechanism to avoid it or stuff it inside. If Harmonizers hide or stuff their anger, it comes out in the form of losing confidence and self-esteem, taking things too personally, and getting depressed because they turn the anger on themselves instead. Inevitably, Harmonizers can't stuff the anger forever. Sometimes they blow up and overreact, then others freak out, confirming their belief that showing anger damages relationships.

"This is what Sam did with me. It was during an executive meeting. I interrupted her and told her to get to the point. She blew up and yelled at me. It was totally out of context and everybody freaked out. Sam felt horrible."

"That's pretty much the story of my life until recently," Kayla responded. "I avoided anger like the plague. And I was the one who ended up depressed."

"Until recently?" Pauline probed.

"Yeah. Lately I've been more willing to tell people when I feel angry. It's less of a problem now. Not that it went away, just that I'm getting better at talking about it instead of stuffing it inside. It still sneaks up on me though, like the other day with Lucas. I totally missed what was happening. I was angry and I wasn't honest with him."

"Great insight! I don't want to oversimplify, but I can say that in my experience the majority of conflicts originate from the Phase issue. Most of us can go through life pretty easily until something happens that brings the Phase issue into focus. Then we have a challenge and a choice to make. Get honest and deal with it openly, or avoid it and head down the path of disconnection and self-sabotage. Self-awareness is rooted in recognizing when this happens. Self-management, then, means we get honest with ourselves and others, and handle it openly."

Kayla checked her understanding. "I can really see how important it is for us to deal authentically with our Phase issue. And I see why you call it doing the hard emotional work."

Pauline added, "Yeah, and it's a lot more scary and vulnerable than safe honesty because we are putting our real stuff on the table. What if someone rejects us? What if they don't take us seriously or don't see the value in our emotions? What if they simply can't relate?"

"Totally. So how do you get over it and get on with the hard emotional work of being honest?" Kayla probed.

"Unfortunately, there's no magic bullet. But there are some affirmations we can give ourselves and others to help things progress. One of the most important affirmations Harmonizers can give themselves is *'My needs and feelings matter. It's okay to express how I feel, and nobody needs to get hurt in the process.'* Another assurance I tell myself regularly is *'How someone responds to me doesn't define me. I choose to speak up because I matter, not because I need someone else's approval.'*"

"Wow, that's powerful stuff. And I bet it's easier said than done," Kayla reflected.

"Yep, no doubt. It takes practice, courage, and faith," Pauline confirmed. "At ProcessCorp one of our commitments is that we support people in talking about their emotional motives and issues. After all, these are what influence us, so why not get it out in the open and support each other in addressing that gap in the most honest way possible?"

"Maybe that's why the interactions between people seem so real and authentic," Kayla wondered to herself.

Pauline broke the silence, "We've only talked about the Harmonizer Phase issue. Every personality type has its own issue. When I first learned about this it blew me away. I'll admit I didn't believe it at first and was stunned that the PCM Profile could reveal this much about me from a few questions. Your PCM Profile identifies which floor is your Phase."

I'M THE SAME AND I'M DIFFERENT

The concept of Phase was not covered in her first training session, but Kayla had looked ahead in her workbook. She saw a little elevator symbol parked next to the Rebel floor in her condo (see Figure 4).

"My Phase floor is Rebel, which is the second floor up in my condo. What's up with that?"

"Have you ever felt you were going through a phase in life? When we say that, we are referring to what's important for us right now during this time frame in our lives. The same is true with personality. One floor in our personality condominium, called our Phase floor, correlates with a few features that are most important right now in our lives. What are they? Motivational needs, distress behavior, and, you guessed it, the emotional issue."

"Hang on. You're losing me." Kayla stopped Pauline. "Before, you said that any of the positive qualities of the different floors in our condo are accessible any time just by riding our elevator. In our first PCM session we learned all about these and practiced riding our elevators up and down to energize different floors. Now you are saying that some qualities are isolated to a certain floor. Which is it?"

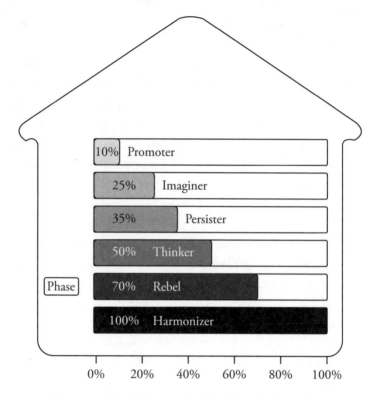

Figure 4. *Kayla's Personality Profile with Phase Floor*

"Ah, yes. This is one of the reasons why I love PCM and why I am so intrigued by it. The phenomenon of Phase explains how we can at the same time have a stable personality throughout our lives, and still experience significant changes in what's important to us and how we behave in distress. It also explains why two people can have the same condo structure yet be so different. It's because their Phase floors are different."

Kayla was beginning to feel a little overwhelmed, but also deeply curious about this phenomenon—particularly because she had recently experienced a pretty dramatic change in what was important to her and hadn't been able to make any sense of it. All that came out of her mouth was, "I don't get it."

Pauline recognized that Kayla's Rebel Phase was running out of energy and needed to recharge if she was going to be able to absorb the rest of their conversation. So she replied with playful energy, "This is heady stuff! We are almost done for today. Let's get up and take a stretch break!"

They walked to the cafeteria and refilled their drinks. After moving around a bit, Kayla was thinking clearly again and ready for the big reveal.

Pauline continued. "Motivational needs, distress behavior, and emotional issues are all connected. You'll learn about that in your next PCM training session. For now, though, it's enough to know that these three things are huge influencers of our behavior. And, at any time in our lives, the needs, distress behavior, and emotional issue of only one floor are the primary driving forces in our lives. This floor is called the Phase. The emotional issue correlated with your Phase is called the Phase issue."

"So our condo structure stays the same throughout our life, but our Phase floor could change?" Kayla checked.

"Yes. This is such an important and unique feature of PCM. Because our condo structure stays the same, our strongest Base Perception and Character Strengths also stay the same. This explains how we stay the same but also change during our lives," Pauline explained.

"You might be too young to have experienced this, but I'll illustrate with an example from my twentieth high school class reunion last fall. At the reception I recognized an old classmate and friend of mine across the room whom I hadn't seen since graduation. We made eye contact and I immediately remembered the connection we had in high school. We were the action kids, always making stuff happen. We made our way to each other and started telling old stories. It was great! But as we shifted to talking about our current lives, I realized that we didn't have much in common at all. Our priorities were really different and the conversation got awkward. We politely moved on to other people. I bet one or both of us had experienced a Phase change since high school. Our motivational needs were different."

"Okay. I get it, in theory. You started with the Harmonizer Phase issue because you said Sam and I had it in common. I noticed that my Harmonizer floor is my Base, and hers is the second one up. Please explain."

"What that means, Kayla, is that our Phase can change. The last piece of the puzzle that Dr. Kahler figured out is this: when we are born and our personality is being formed, our Phase floor is the same as our Base. In other words, the motivators, distress, and Phase issue of our Base floor is primary at birth. We all start there."

"Oh, so that explains why I remember dealing with the Harmonizer Phase issue earlier in my life." Kayla was making connections.

Pauline smiled. "And people change. We go through stuff, we encounter obstacles, we learn and grow. When we don't take good care of ourselves and avoid dealing with our Phase issue, it can initiate a Phase change. The order of our condo doesn't change, but our motivational needs, distress behavior, and Phase issue shift to those of the next floor up in our condo. So, while our condo structure and positive qualities remain unchanged, we begin to experience the world differently because new things are important to us."

"Holy cow! I get it! I've been noticing that my Base Harmonizer needs are still important but not the same as before. You said when people experience a Phase change, they shift to the next floor up. My next floor is Rebel. That's my current Phase floor." Kayla felt more energized.

"Yep," Pauline explained, "Rebel is your current Phase. That means the motivational needs, distress, and Phase issue of your Rebel floor are primary for you right now. Of course, you can still take your elevator to anywhere in your condo and energize the perceptions and character strengths of those floors. But the Rebel floor is especially important for you in terms of your own self-care, leadership style, and ability to connect with others."

"Okay, I have a million questions now! What is the emotional issue for my Rebel Phase? Why did I change to Rebel Phase instead of any other floor in my condo? What do I need to do to stay healthy? How do I determine what Phase other people are in?" Kayla was hungry for more!

"I love your enthusiasm!" Pauline laughed. "These are all the right questions. Feel free to read ahead in your profile. And, good news!

These questions will be answered in your next PCM training module. We are out of time today, but before we end, I will answer one question.

"The Rebel Phase issue is responsibility. This means taking full responsibility for your own emotions and behaviors. The Rebel type is spontaneous, creative, and playful. So, feeling responsible isn't easy, especially when you make a mistake, or fail to meet an expectation. Responsibility is such a buzzkill! What a dilemma!

"So here's your homework. This week I want you to pay attention to situations where you feel responsible and how you handle it. With all the new stuff you are learning every day, I bet you'll have no problem finding examples!"

Kayla immediately felt pressure in her chest, as if she was being squeezed from the outside. She felt like a microscope was being focused on her. She didn't like it at all and wanted to disappear.

Pauline must have noticed. "Don't worry about what's right or wrong, simply pay attention to it. I appreciate and accept you the way you are, mistakes and all! Today we talked about doing the hard emotional work. It's not super fun stuff, but really important. I loved your energy and enthusiasm today. Remember, you are amazing and gifted. I'll be looking forward to hearing what you experience this week."

Kayla felt some of the pressure subside with Pauline's permission and affirmation. "Okay. Got it."

RESOURCE GUIDES

Table 3: Personality Phase Types, Phase Issue, Positive Modus Operandi, and Dilemma

Personality Type	Phase Issue	Positive Modus Operandi	Dilemma
Thinker	Grief	I am a natural planner.	It is my duty to fix things, plan things out, and be sure that there are no surprises. Because of the unpredictable nature of the world, and of people, I lose control of life. Losing things (including time spent) is sad.
Persister	Fear	I am a natural protector.	It is my duty to protect my family, my company, my employees, and my constituency. Because of the unpredictable nature of the world, and of people, I can't always fulfill my duty perfectly. This is frightening.
Harmonizer	Anger	I am a natural caregiver.	It is my duty to show compassion, nurture others, and promote harmony. Because of the nature of humanity, people do mean things, sometimes even on purpose. I feel angry about that.
Rebel	Responsibility	I am a natural funster.	It is my pleasure to enjoy life, play with others, and create new things. Because I make mistakes, and because the world wants to count on me, I experience expectations. I feel responsible and it's very uncomfortable and restrictive.
Imaginer	Autonomy	I am a natural dreamer.	I relish the vast wonder of my imaginative mind and freedom to go there. Because I have to get things done and because people often leave me alone, I feel the pull to get out of my imagination, get into the real world, and get moving. I feel very uncomfortable with this kind of autonomy.
Promoter	Bonding	I am a natural doer.	I take great pride in my self-sufficiency to make things happen and take care of business. Because the world doesn't always move at my pace and people want to get close to me, I feel tied down. Being emotionally reliable and present with another person is very uncomfortable.

In PCM, Phase issues represent the connection between a particular Phase in a person's personality and the emotional issue that is relevant for them at that time in their life. Modus operandi represents the basic approach to life of that personality type. The dilemma is caused by a mismatch between the Phase issue and modus operandi of that personality type.

Table 4: Personality Phase Types, Phase Issue, and Cover-up Behavior

Personality Phase Type	Phase Issue	Cover-up Behavior
Thinker	Grief	Rigid micromanaging, obsessive and compulsive behavior around even the smallest issues of time management, orderliness, and money, and a critical attitude around how lazy and stupid everyone else is
Persister	Fear	Suspicious preoccupation, problems with trust, self-righteous arrogance, and pessimism
Harmonizer	Anger	Losing confidence and self-esteem, taking things too personally, getting depressed, and turning anger on self instead of expressing it assertively
Rebel	Responsibility	Blaming, complaining, sarcasm, and anything else to avoid taking ownership for feelings and behaviors
Imaginer	Autonomy	Avoidance, isolation, and a sense of insignificance
Promoter	Bonding	Negative drama and manipulation to push people away and position self as superior as a way to avoid feeling close

Phase issues and cover-up behavior are correlated. Cover-up behavior is often a sign that a person is not dealing authentically with their Phase issue.

Table 5: Personality Phase Types, Phase Issue, and Affirmations

Personality Phase Type	Phase Issue	Affirmations
Thinker	Grief	It's okay to feel sad when you lose time, opportunity, and relationships. Contrary to what you might think, grieving these losses is the key to regaining your effectiveness as a leader. It's okay to get help if you can't do it on your own.
Persister	Fear	It's okay to feel afraid when you care deeply about protecting your people and organization. Contrary to what you might think, authentically experiencing this fear without attacking anyone is the key to regaining your integrity as a leader. It's okay to get help if you can't do it on your own.
Harmonizer	Anger	It's okay to feel angry when people behave inappropriately to you or the people you care about. Contrary to what you might think, expressing this anger authentically and assertively is the key to regaining your compassion as a leader. It's okay to get help if you can't do it on your own.
Rebel	Responsibility	It's okay to take ownership over things, even if you make mistakes. Contrary to your impulses, owning up to your behavior is the key to regaining your creativity as a leader. It's okay to get help if you can't do it on your own.
Imaginer	Autonomy	It's okay to make autonomous decisions. Claiming your power is the key to regaining your imagination as a leader. It's okay to get help if you can't do it on your own.
Promoter	Bonding	It's okay to get close to the people on whom you depend, as frightening as it might feel. Contrary to your impulses, this is the key to gaining the loyalty and support of your team. It's okay to get help if you can't do it on your own.

Affirmations are self-statements that give permission and guidance around authentic expression of Phase issues. This can often reduce or eliminate the cover-up behavior.

FOUR

Influence

*The test of leadership is not to put greatness into human-
ity, but to elicit it, for the greatness is already there.*
                                                    —James Buchanan

One of the most dangerous things that can happen with personality assessments is entitlement. People learn about their strongest
type or style, embrace it, and then hide behind it. They begin to act
as if their personality entitles them to act in a certain way without
accountability. Here's what entitlement sounds like:

> *"I'm an extrovert so don't be offended by what I say."*
> *"As a High-D, I'm competitive. If you can't hunt with the big dogs,
>   stay on the porch."*
> *"Agreeableness is not one of my strengths, so don't expect me to be
>   sympathetic."*

Part of the problem is how personality assessment results are
portrayed. Any assessment that categorizes types *of* people instead
of describing types *in* people invites entitlement. Most of the problem, however, is how these tools are applied to leadership.

Learning about our personality should help leaders be more responsible, more capable, and more agile. A High-D is not destined

to turn everything into a competition. An extrovert can learn to be sensitive to another's personal space. Empathy and compassion can be learned, even by people with low agreeableness. Personality isn't an entitlement program or get out of jail free card. It's just the opposite. Personality can be the mechanism by which leaders simultaneously honor their uniqueness and influence diverse capabilities and perspectives toward shared goals. Honoring our personality starts with mastering the emotional issues beneath the surface. PCM calls these Phase issues.

It's common wisdom that employees leave their leaders, not their companies. Research reported by the Gallup Organization shows that leaders account for 70 percent of variance in employee engagement.[1] That's a staggering amount of influence.

Positive leadership influence occurs by tapping into people's unique motivational needs and preferred modes of communication. PCM identifies what these are and how to feed them positively. This is a leadership goldmine because employees who are motivated according to their personalities are happier, more engaged, and more productive. Leaders who figure this out and develop the necessary communication and motivation skills can turn their influence into a tremendous lever for business success.

Properly motivating people requires that leaders abandon the Golden Rule in favor of the Platinum Rule. Treating others as I want to be treated is a recipe for disengagement. Treating others as they want to be treated is the key to engagement, especially among a more mobile, discerning, and self-focused workforce. The Platinum Rule requires personality agility, the Golden Rule does not.

One of a leader's most important roles is connecting people with the purpose of an organization. People won't connect with the purpose of an organization unless that purpose connects with their motivational needs. When they can align their Phase motivators with something bigger than themselves, it allows them to apply their personality in ways that make a tremendous positive impact in the world. PCM is a powerful tool to help leaders facilitate these connections.

A resource guide at the end of this chapter shows the preferred communication modes, or channels of communication, for each Base type; the unique motivational needs for each Phase type; and how these needs connect to purpose.

For the rest of the day after her meeting with Pauline, Kayla couldn't stop ruminating about the situation with Pauline and the brochure redesign. She didn't like how she felt when the spotlight was on her and really wanted to blame someone for not giving her the specs ahead of time. Kayla wondered if this might be her unconscious effort to avoid her Phase issue of responsibility. Would she have the courage to be honest with Pauline about it? Did she trust Pauline's promise of safety? Kayla wasn't sure yet.

In the next PCM training session Kayla was fascinated to learn about parts and channels, the specific verbal and nonverbal behaviors that go into effective communication. She learned that communication is defined as "an offer and acceptance in the same channel." It made sense that unless people are on the same wavelength, and unless the message is received as intended, communication isn't happening. Based on this definition, Kayla could see that very few interactions actually meet the criteria for communication, and why so many interactions turn into miscommunication, especially via texting and email. Her Thinker floor appreciated how predictable and observable it all is once you know what to look for. Her Harmonizer Base floor was encouraged to have a method to connect authentically with each person by meeting them where they are at in the current moment. Her Persister floor valued this new framework for respecting people by adapting how we interact with them. Her Imaginer floor could see endless possibilities for improving relationships in her own life.

Although there was a lot of technical learning, what helped Kayla the most were simple words Sandy, their trainer, used to describe the five channels of communication: Telling, Asking, Caring, Playing, and Protecting. Each personality type has a preferred channel that is most effective, and a least preferred channel that will most likely invite miscommunication and distress. The preferred channel of her Base Harmonizer was Caring, a channel that invites others to feel nurtured and cared for. That felt just right to Kayla. The preferred channel for her Rebel Phase was Playing, which also matched her experience. "No wonder I like it when people say kind things to me or joke around," Kayla realized.

Kayla also learned a bit more about Phase changes, and they practiced how to motivate each personality Phase. Her PCM Profile included an action plan with specific guidance on how to get her needs met in healthy ways. It was spot-on. Kayla was shocked by how accurate the PCM Profile was, and how it fit for each person in her class.

The next week involved lots of new learning. ProcessCorp had taken on several new corporate clients and Kayla got to be involved in some of the initial exploration sessions around the culture, goals, and aspirations of these clients. She was much more aware of how Pauline and others in her department were adapting their communication based on the person with whom they were communicating. They talked openly about it and tested out their hunches with each other. They talked about how they were feeling, and it was remarkable how vulnerable it seemed to Kayla. In her previous jobs, getting vulnerable about feelings was the last thing anybody felt safe doing.

And it wasn't gushy, touchy-feely stuff that crossed boundaries. It was genuine and helpful. One of her teammates, Mario, shared his feeling of sadness when the client didn't select his brand story concept. "I put a lot of work into it and I feel sad that it wasn't chosen." Several people empathized with him. Pauline said, "I hear you. It's okay to feel sad when something you have worked for doesn't go as planned. I know you want to make sense of it and can't. How can we best support you? You are smart and I bet you'll connect some dots for the future."

Kayla wasn't used to this level of support and affirmation. Although she was working to focus only on her own Phase issue of responsibility, she couldn't help but wonder if sadness was connected to Mario's personality Phase in some way.

IS IT OKAY TO BE HONEST WITH YOU?

When Kayla arrived for their next session, Pauline was standing in the doorway to her office. "Hey, I need to get some fresh air. What say we talk at the coffee shop around the corner?"

Kayla was excited. The boss wanted to take her out for coffee? She thought that was pretty special. "Sure!"

Once they got their drinks and were settled in a quiet corner of the coffee shop, Pauline asked Kayla, "I'm curious, Kayla, what did you notice this week about your Phase issue?"

Kayla felt the pressure in her chest. She knew what she needed to do but was anxious. "Can I be honest with you, Pauline?" Kayla asked tentatively.

"Absolutely, Kayla," Pauline reassured. "I meant what I said last week about accepting you the way you are. It's safe to be open with me and I will not judge you. Our commitment to interaction safety at ProcessCorp is a sacred one."[2]

"Okay, thanks for that reassurance," Kayla began. "Do you remember a couple of weeks ago when you asked me to redo that brochure design?"

"Vaguely. Why do you ask?" Pauline was curious.

"I think I bumped up against my Phase issue that day. I felt embarrassed and hated feeling accountable for not getting it right. Although I agreed with you and didn't argue, inside I was feeling like it wasn't my fault. I wanted to blame you for not giving me clear directions in the first place. I wanted to run away from it all."

Pauline smiled knowingly, and responded with a playful tone, "Wow, I totally get how hard that must have been. Yikes!"

Kayla continued, grateful for not being judged by Pauline, "I definitely don't like when the spotlight is on me, especially when I make a mistake or don't do something quite right. Don't get me wrong, I love figuring stuff out and I want to please people, but I just don't like the pressure of expectations and scrutiny."

"Yep, that definitely stinks! Did you notice anything about how you reacted to this feeling?" Pauline asked.

Kayla explained what she had learned about herself. "I've noticed that when I feel responsible, I have this immediate urge to make an excuse or blame someone. I want to run away from the feeling and if I can find someone else or something else to blame, I can get away from it. I'm not proud of it. I don't usually act on the urge, but I can get a pretty negative attitude inside and it probably shows."

"Kayla, that's perfectly normal and it's part of your personality," Pauline's voice was reassuring. "Every person in the world with a Rebel Phase has felt like that, and every one of them has acted on the urge from time to time. It's human."

"What a relief!" Kayla sighed. "Tell Lucas that. He hates it when I blame or make excuses."

"I hate to take sides, Kayla, but I think Lucas is right on this one." Pauline waited for Kayla's reaction. Kayla seemed curious.

PERSONALITY IS NOT AN ENTITLEMENT PROGRAM

Pauline continued, "It's not okay to make excuses or blame others for your behaviors and feelings. There's a big difference between how we feel and acting on how we feel; in other words, the distance between stimulus and response. One of the most valuable emotional intelligence skills is the ability to identify emotions and use them to guide effective action, but not be ruled by them."

Kayla felt bold today, so she pressed the issue. "What do you mean? This is my personality and it is part of me. Lucas should accept it just like I accept his opinionated skepticism, right?"

Pauline smiled. "Your Phase issue is part of you and it's okay to be uncomfortable with the feeling of responsibility. That doesn't mean you aren't responsible for your actions. Everyone is 100 percent responsible for their feelings, thoughts, and actions. Regardless of where they come from or what happened, it is still our responsibility what we do with them."

Kayla didn't like how she felt when hearing this, but she knew it was true. Instead of arguing, Kayla tried to reflect what she was learning through a joke. "So are you saying that personality is not an entitlement program?"

Pauline laughed spontaneously, so loud that several people near them turned to see what was going on. "That's hilarious and so true, Kayla! I've always said that personality isn't a get out of jail free card, but I like this much better. Can I use it?"

Personality is not an entitlement program.

"Sure! What I really want to know is how to handle my discomfort with responsibility in a healthier way."

"Easier said than done, as usual," Pauline chuckled, "but not that complicated. You've already completed step one, be aware and own it. Step two is to share it openly and honestly. This may seem totally crazy to tell someone you don't like responsibility, but here's the twist. Just because you don't like it doesn't mean you can't take ownership and figure it out. Step three is to ask for help. This sends a clear message that you are capable and willing to learn and grow. Step four is to use your unique personality to solve the problem in front of you. Each floor in your condo has unique character strengths that you can access to help you. You have a special set of skills that you can use to turn that negative energy into something super cool."

Kayla had a knack for playing with words. "I got it, Pauline. Feel it, share it, ask for help, solve it with your special set of skills."

Four Steps for Dealing with a Phase Issue
1. Feel it
2. Share it
3. Ask for help
4. Solve it using your special set of skills

"Fabulous! You nailed it again. That last part sounds like a line from a famous movie. What a terrific mantra. This is the process anyone can use to see themselves through when the Phase issue comes knocking."

Something else clicked for Kayla. "Wow, that's exactly what happened with you and Mario the other day!" She blurted out. "You guided him through all four steps." Kayla also tested her theory about sadness and confirmed that is the Phase issue for the Thinker personality type.

"Right on, Kayla. It's fantastic how you're rockin' this!" Pauline congratulated.

"Thanks." Kayla felt energized. "So what are we covering today?"

MOTIVATION

"Today is about influence," Pauline replied. "One of the most important functions of a leader is to influence people toward the team and organizational goals. Seeing people through means influencing them in a way that honors each person for how they are built by leveraging their personality. Seeing ourselves through means influencing ourselves to show up each day in the best space possible."

Kayla was curious, "Does this have anything to do with motivation?"

"Yes, it does," Pauline affirmed. "It has everything to do with motivation. As you learned in your last PCM training session, every personality type has unique, inborn psychological needs that must be satisfied in order to function at our best. These are called motivators because we are intrinsically driven to satisfy these needs and when they are satisfied we have more energy to interact with positive energy and enthusiasm."

"I also learned that the most important motivators for me at this time in my life are those of my Phase floor," Kayla added, "and that these have changed at some point in my life from Harmonizer to Rebel."

"Yes, and there's more!" Pauline added. "When people experience a Phase change, these new motivators become primary, and the motivators of our Base floor become secondary. It's like they fade into the background but are still important."

Kayla felt compelled to explore something else she had learned about Phase and Phase changes. "Sandy said that everyone starts out with their Phase being the same as their Base floor in their condo, and that two-thirds of the population experience one or more Phase changes in their life. My current Rebel Phase is the next floor up in my condo. Is this typical?"

"Yes, Kayla," Pauline answered. "Did Sandy tell you about how we always go to the next floor, never skip a floor, and never go back?"

"She did, and that blows my mind! How does this work? How does the PCM Profile know?" Kayla was incredulous.

"I have no idea, Kayla," Pauline matched Kayla's surprise. "It's all about developmental psychology and the nature–nurture process, about which I know very little."

"Well, in any case, I agree that I've experienced a Phase change. It seems like I'm a lot more on the move these days. I can't sit still as long, and I get restless. One of the things I love about working here is that I have flexibility to move around when I want to and I get to work on novel problems every day."

"That's awesome! Tell me more." Pauline used the Playing channel with Kayla, but resorted to her own favorite channel, Telling, in the very next sentence, as is typical with people when they become passionate about the content of a conversation.

Kayla didn't mind. She felt energized and her elevator was moving freely, so she was able to respond effortlessly to Pauline's directive, even though it required her to go to the sixth floor in her condo. "My current Rebel Phase motivator is contact. That means I am motivated by movement. Making contact with people and things is energizing because it keeps the creativity flowing. It doesn't have to be loud or wild, as long as there's positive energy."

Pauline probed further, "How about the suggestions in your PCM Profile action plan? Did they resonate?"

"Most of them did," Kayla shared. "I highlighted the ones that I liked the most: a relaxed work environment, permission to move around, variety in my work, and being with people. Oh yeah, and plenty of music and colors don't hurt, either!"

"That's awesome," Pauline said with a grin. I'm curious how easily you are able to get contact motivation here at ProcessCorp. I know it's only been three weeks, but how's it going?"

Kayla reflected for a moment. "Actually, it's amazing. Now that we are talking about it, I realize that the people around me have been offering and encouraging contact all along without me even knowing it. We have music in our office. It seems someone is always inviting me to take a walk to the cafeteria or head outside during break. We even have this game going where we try to guess where in their personalities our customers are coming from and share what's working to connect with them. The novelty and creative problem-solving of my job really fills my tank. The more comfortable I get, the more I've been taking it upon myself to do these things."

"I'm so glad to hear that, Kayla," Pauline said enthusiastically. "How is it working?"

"I love it. I look forward to coming to work, I enjoy being here, and I feel like you all accept me for who I am."

"What about your attitude toward your work and our company?" Pauline's tone was more serious.

"It's huge, Pauline. I care a lot more about what we are doing than I've ever cared about work. I have no problem working hard because I feel satisfied when I can contribute. I feel like I'm part of a team and we are working together to delight our customers. Yeah, I'm tired at the end of the day, but it's so much better than feeling drained!"

"I'm really glad to hear that. I'd like to share with you some research we've been doing at ProcessCorp related to motivation." Pauline pulled a packet out of her briefcase. "Since we got serious about applying PCM in our culture, we've been tracking the connection between motivation and our key performance indicators; most importantly, customer satisfaction and retention, employee engagement, and our financial performance.

"We define motivation like this: Are employees getting their motivational needs met at work in a healthy way that coexists with other people's motivators? By now you are probably getting a sense for how we implement this in everyday behaviors. It's a pretty intentional process. First, we get a PCM Profile for each person when they are hired, just like we did with you. This lets us know where to focus our efforts. Then, we check in about how it's going. We talk to employees about their Phase motivators and work with them to get those satisfied in healthy ways every day. We hold managers accountable for having these conversations and working with employees on it. And, as part of our employee engagement survey, we ask people to rate how well their motivators are being satisfied at work. This, along with daily conversations about our personalities in a safe and inclusive environment, creates a powerful, self-improving feedback loop."

Kayla was curious. "Now I'm going to ride my elevator to my Thinker floor and ask a data question. So what does your research say?"

"Glad you asked, Kayla." Pauline beamed with pride and pulled out two pieces of paper in plastic protectors, each with charts on them. "The data is pretty impressive. Every single year since we implemented PCM in our culture, we've seen steady positive growth in our key performance indicators. As motivation improves, so does business success. We've done our best to track the actual cost of profiles, materials, training, and time so we can calculate return on investment.

"Before we started using PCM, our turnover was about 15 percent. The first year we trained and coached our C-level executives and top managers in PCM: about 30 people. The following year, turnover had dropped to 12.5 percent. This is significant, because it costs about one third of an employee's salary to replace them. We employ about 250 people, so our savings was over $100,000.[3] That's twice what we spent on the training and coaching, which calculates to a 200 percent return on investment, or ROI. We also saw improvements in engagement and customer retention, which are hard to put a value on. I know one of the clients we saved was totally because PCM helped us recognize and correct a pattern of miscommunication that was heading for disaster. Best we can figure, we get about 300 percent ROI. That means for every dollar we spend on

PCM training and implementation in our culture, we get about three dollars improvement in value."

Pauline pointed to the second graph. "You'll see that ROI started a bit lower and increased steadily over the first six years. That's when we were figuring out how to fully integrate PCM into our culture. It seems like every day we find new ways to live out the incredible potential of PCM, and the rewards are so satisfying."

"ROI is a fairly squishy thing to measure when it comes to leadership and people skills, isn't it?" Kayla was skeptical.

"Yes, Kayla, it is," Pauline agreed. "We do our best to measure it and we are pretty confident that it's making a difference. Plus, it's the right thing to do."

"You said PCM improved employee engagement?" Kayla asked.

"Our engagement numbers are in the 98th percentile, according to Gallup. How do you think we made the 'Top Places to Work' list?" Pauline chuckled.

Kayla could tell how proud Pauline was to share the data, and assumed it was related to Pauline's Thinker Phase. Kayla had learned that the Thinker Phase is motivated by recognition of productive work and time structure. Kayla was curious to learn more. She tried a strategy she had learned in class: connect with a person using their Base channel and Perception, and motivate them according to their Phase needs. Kayla used the Telling channel first, followed by recognition of Pauline's work. "Tell me more about your Thinker Phase. You've contributed a lot of hard work that went into those numbers you shared."

Pauline lit up. "Thanks, Kayla. I am really proud of our company and our team. It has been a lot of work and it's very rewarding to see the numbers to prove it. For me, recognition of productive work means I need to know that I am getting the most important stuff done. I thrive on task lists, goals, and metrics. Time structure means I need to know I'm using my time efficiently. Each night when I go to bed, I ask myself if I have used my time productively to accomplish things that help ProcessCorp function more efficiently. One of the reasons I like PCM so much is that it reveals the method to the madness; it unpacks the mechanisms behind why people act the way they do, shows what to look for, and gives us specific strategies to be more effective."

"I can certainly see how your Phase motivators inspire you to do great work and lead a well-run department. What was it like for you before Thinker became your Phase?" Kayla was curious about what motivated the Promoter, which was Pauline's Base floor.

Pauline answered, "When I started at ProcessCorp, I was in a Promoter Phase. I was motivated by incidence—a lot of excitement in short bursts of time. My whole life I loved risk, excitement, competition, and the thrill of the chase. I played sports, was the star of the school play, and was the president of the student council in college.

"Most of my professional life before ProcessCorp was in sales. It was pretty competitive but I loved it. It was also cutthroat. Unfortunately, I spent many years doing whatever it took to get ahead, even if that meant undercutting others in the process. I didn't let myself get close to anyone, and even ruined my first marriage because I cared more about my next commission than my husband. That's the dark side of Promoter. I wasn't taking care of my needs in a healthy way, and I wasn't dealing with my Phase issue of bonding. I avoided intimacy and I used manipulation and negative drama to put distance between me and the people who cared about me the most.

"It was after my husband left me and I got fired from my job as a sales executive that I hit rock bottom. It took me a while to realize that I was 100 percent responsible for my feelings, thoughts, and behaviors. I realized that unless I could authentically experience emotional closeness with another person, I was going to be alone the rest of my life. I didn't want that. So I got some professional help and worked on it.

"Long story short, after I dealt authentically with my Phase issue, I noticed a change in my motivators. I was much less interested in competition, and much more interested in achievement. I was up at the crack of dawn planning my day and setting goals. I'd never really thought beyond the next sale, and suddenly I was using the calendar and list-making apps on my phone! I guess that was the emergence of my Thinker Phase."

"Sounds like things got pretty bad before they got better," Kayla empathized.

"Yeah," Pauline agreed. "That's usually how it goes. When we don't get our motivational needs met in healthy ways and we don't deal authentically with our Phase issue, things can get pretty dark. Most of the time, this type of distress and dysfunction are what lead up to Phase changes. It's not pretty but it's what I needed to go through at the time. Thank goodness for Sam."

"Sam? What did Sam have to do with it?" Kayla was confused.

"Sam saved my life, Kayla." Pauline was silent for a while. "Sam hired me to work in the Storytelling and Brand Engagement department. I had applied for an opening here and didn't expect to get called in for an interview. My life was a mess. When I did get the invite, it was Sam who interviewed me. Sam told me that she saw so much potential in me, and that she believed in me and wanted to mentor me. I was scared to death. I wanted to burn the place down. But I remembered my therapist's voice in my head challenging me to embrace intimacy instead of run away from it. So I took the job."

"So, what did Sam do next?" Kayla asked.

"Sam gave me what any distressed Promoter needs more than anything else: strong boundaries and unconditional acceptance. She didn't put up with my crap, but she also never rejected me. It was the weirdest thing because I always expected that if you got close to someone, they'd take advantage of you. So I was used to self-protection. Strangely, though, this is what it took for me to start opening up and get healthy. I had nowhere to hide, and had to take full responsibility for myself. Sam treated me with compassion and helped me recognize that I was valuable, capable, and responsible."

"That's intense, Pauline. Thanks for sharing."

"Absolutely, Kayla. I actually enjoy telling my Phase change story because it reminds me and others of how important it is to get our Phase needs met in a healthy way, and deal authentically with our Phase issue. These are foundational to leadership. It can get pretty personal and intense, but if we don't have a place to talk about it and help each other out, the alternative is pretty grim."

Now Kayla was even more curious about her own Phase change, but before she could ask Pauline about it, a friendly "hello" interrupted their conversation. It was Sam, who had just ordered a coffee and come over to where they were sitting.

Sam asked, "Am I interrupting anything?"

"Not at all," Kayla and Pauline replied in unison. Pauline continued, "Want to join us? We were just talking about influence, motivation, and my Phase change story."

Sam looked at her watch. "I've got a few minutes before my next appointment. I'd love to join you. I love Phase change stories!"

THE PROBLEM WITH THE GOLDEN RULE

"Perfect timing," Pauline said enthusiastically. "Kayla, Sam taught me two very important lessons about motivation and influence. Maybe she would share them with you, too. Sam, would you be willing to tell Kayla your philosophy about the Golden Rule and purpose?"

"Absolutely," Sam began. "The first one has to do with the Golden Rule. I was brought up to believe that you should treat others like you want to be treated. I did a pretty good job of that. In my previous career, I was in a Thinker Phase and I gave everyone around me what I would have wanted: plenty of data, time frames, and the logical reason for everything. When I didn't get the results I wanted, I turned up the volume. When that didn't work, I turned on people because I decided they were stupid and lazy and didn't deserve to benefit from my experience and expertise. It became a vicious and self-destructive cycle.

Influence Lesson #1: Treating people like you want to be treated can backfire when they have different motivational needs. Treating them like they want to be treated is much more effective.

"By the time I founded ProcessCorp I was in my Harmonizer Phase. Still clinging to the Golden Rule, I treated everyone like I wanted to be treated. I showed compassion and empathy, offered compliments, and tried to make sure everyone felt cared for and nurtured. Some people loved it! When I look back now, I realize the ones who loved it were other people in a Harmonizer Phase or with lots of Harmonizer energy in their personality. But others didn't seem to respond at all. Some people began avoiding me. Others openly criticized me for being a bleeding heart and too soft to lead a company. I remember someone comparing me to Jimmy Carter and saying I should go start a nonprofit service organization.

"I responded by doubling down on compassion. More caring, more personal notes, more creature comforts. When that didn't work, I started questioning myself. What was wrong with me? Was I even cut out to be a leader? At the same time, I was really angry at people for not appreciating all I did for them. Of course, I didn't express it.

"I remember sharing my concerns with my executive coach, and I'll never forget what she said. She asked me, 'Samantha, why are you being so selfish?' I felt insulted and nearly got up and left. Thankfully my coach had more to say. 'You are treating everyone like *you* want to be treated. You are projecting your motivational needs onto everyone else. Some of them share those same motivators and that's great. But for those who aren't motivated like you, your nurturing behavior is demotivating, maybe even offensive to them. You can't treat everyone like you want to be treated. You've got to treat them like *they* want to be treated.'

"I can still remember the heaviness in my gut, and shame I felt as I let it soak in. All this time I was pushing my motivators onto others. Selfish indeed! Thankfully, my coach understood seeing people through and offered me reassurance. 'Your heart is in the right place, Sam.' She said, 'You care deeply about people feeling seen and valued. And, you have a great tool to help you do this in ways that work for them. You've been talking about PCM and it seems there could be some wisdom there.'

"That's when it clicked for me. The Platinum Rule: Treat others as *they* want to be treated. 'I can do that,' I said to myself. When I shared my epiphany with my leadership team, they weren't that impressed, but were kind about it."

Pauline interrupted Sam and looked at Kayla, "Yeah, I remember that. We all wondered when she would figure this out."

The Platinum Rule: Treat others as *they* want to be treated.

Sam laughed, leaned back in her chair and took a sip of her coffee. Kayla wanted to test out what she had gleaned from Sam's story. "So the lesson is that motivation is the key to influence, and people are motivated differently, so seeing people through means treating them as they want to be treated, not how I want to be treated. Am I on track?"

"I couldn't have said it better myself. Most leaders talk the talk, but very few have developed the curiosity, humility, and skill to really put it into practice. In my previous career we profiled and analyzed people and had all this information, but did nothing about it. What's the point in that?"

THE PROBLEM WITH PURPOSE

Sam looked at her watch again. "I've still got a few minutes, so here goes. The second lesson is about purpose. Purpose is really important to me but my understanding of it has evolved a lot. I used to think that purpose was about discovering where you can fit in to make a difference in the world. That's great, but over time I began to realize that it's bigger than that. Purpose is about something bigger than you. It's about finding a reason beyond yourself to be more and do more, finding your 'why.' There's a lot of research showing how important purpose is at work. Authors like John Izzo and Dan Pink have written terrific books on the power of purpose.[4] A lot of companies have invested great amounts of energy in identifying mission, vision, and values as a way to clarify purpose and connecting employees to that purpose. It's true that people who are connected to the mission are more engaged and loyal. Just look at successful companies like Disney, Patagonia, or Walmart."

Kayla replied, "I know what you are talking about. I remember at the hospital we had this big initiative to drive the mission to the front lines. A consultant was brought in to help our executive team and board refine the mission, vision, and values. Then it was posted everywhere. We even got new employee badges with a bullet point summary printed on the back."

"Wow, that's pretty serious," Sam said semisarcastically.

"Truthfully, it didn't work for me," Kayla admitted. "I thought it was dumb. Not that I disagreed with what it said, just that it didn't connect with me."

No sooner had the words come out of her mouth than Kayla had a light-bulb moment. "I didn't connect to the purpose because the purpose didn't connect to my motivators. I wish I had figured that out a lot sooner!"

Sam took another sip of her coffee. "I did about the same thing as the hospital where you worked before. Lots of energy identifying the mission, vision, and values. Lots of energy trying to push it across the organization and not much buy-in.

"That's the second lesson I learned. Motivation is the foundation for purpose. Unless people are motivated according to their Phase motivators, they don't have the mental, psychological, or spiritual energy to think about purpose. However, when they can see a connection between their unique motivators and the big picture, it's like opening the floodgates of engagement and productivity."

"You've cracked the code, Sam! That's brilliant." Kayla was inspired.

Influence Lesson #2: People won't connect with purpose unless purpose connects with their motivators.

"Well, I don't know about that." Sam was reserved but confident. "But I am certain of this: people want to be part of something bigger than themselves. It's built into us. People are also unique based on their Phase motivators. When they can align their Phase motivators with something bigger than themselves, it allows them to apply their personality in ways that make a tremendous positive impact in the world. Even better, it's intrinsically rewarding because nothing feels better than getting my needs met and using my strengths to make a difference."

Kayla couldn't help herself. She put her fist up for a fist bump. Sam reciprocated and they "blew it up" as both women pulled their hands backward and laughed.

Sam got up. "I gotta go. Thanks for inviting me to join you."

INFLUENCE

Pauline put her empty coffee mug down on the table with a thud. "Now that's influence! And, the best part is that it taps into the individual, collective, and transcendental aspects of our existence. We are individuals. We also coexist in society with others who are different. Together we are better and can transcend our limitations to achieve some pretty amazing stuff."

As Pauline was putting the charts back in her briefcase, she reflected, "Sometimes I think back to when I was growing up. Imagine if our parents, teachers, and coaches had taken this approach with us! What if instead of trying to make us into replicas of themselves, or push their own motivators on everyone, or create learning environments that only support a couple of the personality types, they would have focused on teaching us to get our own motivators met. What if they would have helped us connect our motivators with the big picture and guide us in using our unique gifts to make the biggest difference in the world?"

"I can't even imagine. The world would be a different place. People would be happier and more fulfilled, and I bet we could solve much bigger problems together." Kayla had mixed feelings. She wondered what would have been different for her.

After a long pause, Pauline spoke up. "It's easy to look back and wonder 'what if.' The good news is that we can do it differently in the future. Seeing people through can start right now.

"Speaking of which, I have two homework assignments for you. First, I want you to research MUSE School in Calabasas, California.[5] Since 2010, this school has dedicated itself to seeing students through using PCM. It's the only school in the world where PCM is completely integrated into the culture. What they are doing is truly revolutionary. They are educating today the children who will change the world tomorrow. The things they are doing can apply to any organization. And they are helping other schools implement the same principles.

"The second assignment is to focus on influence this week. Reflect on influences from your past and how they connected with your personality. Consider your own motivators and special strengths. How do they line up with our purpose here at ProcessCorp, as well as your own purpose in life? How could you exert greater influence by helping others do the same?"

Kayla and Pauline walked back to the office humming tunes for their new mantra on Phase issues: "Feel it, share it, ask for help, solve it with your special set of skills."

RESOURCE GUIDE

Table 6: Personality Base Type, Preferred Communication Channel, and Implications for Leadership

Personality Base Type	Preferred Communication Channel	Implications for Leadership
Thinker	Requestive *Asking*	The Requestive channel is a mode of communication that uses questions and answers to exchange data and information. Thinker Base types prefer to be asked about their thoughts. They prefer a Democratic leadership style that invites their ideas. Using the Directive channel with them can invite stress and miscommunication.
Persister	Requestive *Asking*	The Requestive channel is a mode of communication that uses questions and answers to exchange data and information. Persister Base types prefer to be asked about their opinions. They prefer a Democratic leadership style that invites their opinions. Using the Directive channel with them can invite stress and miscommunication.
Harmonizer	Nurturative *Caring*	The Nurturative channel is a mode of communication that uses empathy and validation to invite someone to feel nurtured and cared for. Harmonizer Base types prefer to be nurtured for who they are as a person and share feelings. They prefer a Benevolent leadership style focused on how people are feeling. Using the Directive channel with them can invite stress and miscommunication.
Rebel	Emotive *Playing*	The Emotive channel is a mode of communication that uses playful exchanges to keep things lively and upbeat. Rebel Base types want to have fun and enjoy humor. They prefer a Laissez-Faire leadership style allowing them the freedom to be creative. Using the Directive channel with them can invite stress and miscommunication.
Imaginer	Directive *Telling*	The Directive channel is a mode of communication that uses directives to elicit behavior. Imaginer Base types prefer to be told what to do. They prefer an Autocratic leadership style that clarifies directives then allows time and space to execute. Using the Requestive channel with them can invite stress and miscommunication.
Promoter	Directive *Telling*	The Directive channel is a mode of communication that uses directives to elicit behavior. Promoter Base Types prefer to be told what to do. They are activated by an Autocratic leadership style that gets to the point and makes things happen. Using the Requestive channel with them can invite stress and miscommunication.

FIVE

Self-Deception

Stop lying to yourself. When we deny our own truth, we deny our own potential.

—Steve Maraboli

Learning about personality differences, especially when you know how to adapt communication accordingly, enables much greater influence than most people are used to. This is uncomfortable for many leaders because the last thing we want to do is manipulate people, or treat them like a puzzle to figure out so we can get what we want.

Positive leadership is about influencing individual strengths toward shared goals. When people get their Phase needs met in positive ways and help others do the same, they can exert positive influence. When people don't get their Phase needs met in healthy ways, they will attempt to get those very same needs met negatively, with or without awareness, and this is called distress. Influence is about getting needs met positively. Manipulation is about getting needs met negatively. We all know that negative attention can have great influence as well. Many workplaces and personal relationships are ruled by the influence of negative attention.

> Influence is about getting needs met positively. Manipulation is about getting needs met negatively.

Distress is all about deception and justification. It starts with deceiving ourselves about who is worthwhile and under what conditions. We spend enormous energy trying to justify our beliefs about our own and others' value, capability, and responsibility, and behave in a manner that fulfills those prophecies. This is why our distress invites distress from others. Leaders in distress can't see the forest for the trees because they are focused on proving their version of reality instead of positively motivating themselves and others.

Toxic leaders spend all their energy trying to control negative behavior and feel justified. Despite how hard they try, they can't get a handle on the problem because they aren't dealing with the root cause. PCM reveals that behind every negative attention behavior is an unmet positive need.

Leaders can apply this four-step process to maintain positive influence and avoid the dangers of self-deception.

1. Recognize their own negative attention distress warning signs.
2. Arrange to get their Phase needs met positively every day.
3. Recognize others' distress warning signs.
4. Offer others their positive Phase needs on a regular basis.

Resource guides at the end of this chapter show the early warning signs and negative attention behavior associated with each unmet positive need, as well as the best and worst workplace environments to motivate each Phase type.

Kayla was on cloud nine for the rest of the day. As soon as she got home, she searched the internet for MUSE School in Calabasas, California. She learned about the dream of two sisters with a vision for passion-based learning and care for the environment. Their motto was pretty aspirational: "Inspiring and preparing young people to live consciously with themselves, one another, and the planet." She was impressed with how intentional this school was in building PCM into every facet of their program.

Kayla discovered that every teacher and staff member is trained to recognize and respond to every personality type within their students, and each other. PCM classes are even offered for parents and caregivers. They create space for all types to learn according to their motivational needs. They teach students how to communicate with all the personality types. They even let students tell teachers how they want to be communicated with during the day. They hold students to high standards, as evidenced by meeting state accreditation standards and graduating successful classes of college entrants. Every student has a learning plan that includes their personality structure, how they are getting their needs met, and how they can learn best. And, the teachers honor the personality diversity within their team as well. Behavior problems are virtually nonexistent.

INFLUENCES FROM MY PAST

Kayla decided to go for a bike ride on a new trail she had been wanting to explore. She loaded up her bike and headed out. Kayla wished she had been able to go to a school like MUSE. She wondered how she had been influenced by her parents, friends, and teachers. She reflected on her favorite teacher, Mrs. Panetta, from fifth grade. Mrs. Panetta always gave her a hug in the morning. She was patient and kind when Kayla struggled in class and was always so warm and affirming during parent-teacher conferences. "No wonder I liked Mrs. Panetta!" Kayla realized. "She offered me my Harmonizer Phase needs every day."

Mr. Fredricks was a different story. Kayla hated math in school, and it started with Mr. Fredricks. He was nonemotional, didn't look people in the eye, and never seemed to care. He got excited about math but didn't have compassion for Kayla when she was anxious or confused. When she asked for help, Mr. Fredricks would ask rhetorical questions or refer her back to the workbook. Kayla often felt stupid and small. She quit asking for help from the teacher and decided that math wasn't for her.

Kayla's mom wasn't much help growing up. She worked nights in the laundry department of a hospital. Although she provided for the family and took care of the essentials, she wasn't present. She was either tired or asleep much of the time that Kayla was in the house.

Kayla's dad was a funster, always playing pranks, telling jokes, and having a good time. He worked as a mechanic for a large trucking company. He also played in a band with a few of his coworkers. They would practice in the garage and play occasional gigs on the weekends. Although Kayla enjoyed the lively atmosphere, she often wished dad would spend more quality time with her. More recently, though, Kayla had noticed how much more she was connecting with her dad.

A steep section on the trail jolted Kayla from her daydreaming. After navigating the hill, she stopped for a water break. While she was soaking in the cool evening air and beautiful view from the hill, Kayla had an epiphany. "It's because of my Phase change! My dad is probably in a Rebel Phase and that's my second floor. Growing up, my Harmonizer Phase wanted a more personal connection, but now that my Phase has changed to Rebel, my interactions with him fill my tank more. That's because I'm motivated differently. He hasn't changed . . . I have!"

When Kayla got home she was excited to tell Lucas about her day and what she'd realized on her bike ride. Lucas surprised her with Chinese takeout.

APPLYING THE PLATINUM RULE

Lucas was curious to hear about what Kayla had learned from Pauline. Kayla was so excited to share about the Platinum Rule, the strategy for dealing with her Phase issue, and what an impact PCM had on ProcessCorp's business success.

Eventually though, Lucas did what he always did: played devil's advocate, a typical posture for persons in a Persister Phase. After all, they are natural protectors, on the lookout for danger and sniffing out inconsistencies.

"That all sounds great in theory, Kayla. I don't doubt that people are happier when you give them what they want. I mean, who isn't? But how realistic is that? People can't expect to get their motivational needs met all the time. Sometimes you gotta just deal with it and push through even when things aren't easy. That's the problem with this generation, they expect to have everything their way."

Kayla felt defensive. Instead of defending herself or taking sides though, she tried to put herself in Lucas's shoes by energizing her own Persister perception of Opinions, and connecting with the strengths of being conscientious, dedicated, and observant. "Lucas has a lot of Persister energy," she reminded herself. "He sees the world through the lens of values. He admires qualities like perseverance, integrity, and character, so I can imagine this all seems kind of fluffy to him. I wonder if this is his current Phase."

Kayla realized that if she wanted to influence Lucas in a positive way, the conversation had to connect with his motivators, not hers. She had learned in PCM training that people in a Persister Phase are motivated by recognition of purposeful work and respect for their convictions. This fit for Lucas. He seemed most satisfied when he knew his work made a meaningful difference and was done with quality. His work was a reflection of his character and values. So Kayla gave it a try.

"Lucas, I can completely see where you are coming from. This all seems pretty fluffy, like anything goes, as long as people are happy. I'm remembering something I said to Pauline earlier today and I wonder if it would resonate with you. Pauline and Sam were pushing me to take ownership over my discomfort with responsibility, reminding me that regardless of my personality, I am responsible for my feelings, thoughts, and behaviors. My conclusion was that personality is not an entitlement program. How does that sit with you?"

"That's exactly what I'm saying, Kayla." Lucas seemed almost jubilant. "I have no problem with supporting diversity and all that, but people still have to step up and get the work done."

Kayla was excited about the connection she was making with Lucas. "I'm with you. The main takeaway for me is that we have to balance individual differences with our collective goals and purpose. When people are treated according to their own personality, they have more energy and enthusiasm to contribute toward the big goals. They do higher quality work because they are invested."

"I can buy that," Lucas said calmly. "I'll be curious to see how it plays out with you. I have noticed that you seem happier, and you aren't making excuses as much."

"Yeah. I hate to admit it, but I am happier," Kayla agreed. "I'm realizing that if I feel it, share it, ask for help, and solve it with my special set of skills, I'm much better off." Kayla felt a new level of confidence.

"So Kayla, what motivates you?" Lucas asked.

"Thanks for asking. Let's clean up dinner and head to the balcony and I'll tell you!" Kayla felt a deeper connection with Lucas and was excited about his curiosity. She used her PCM action plan to tell Lucas about her Base and Phase motivational needs.

MEETING PEOPLE WHERE THEY ARE AT

Kayla spent a good deal of time thinking about how her personality structure and most developed character strengths could help her contribute at ProcessCorp. She could see how her warm and welcoming style and creative energy were valuable for her work. It wasn't difficult for her to accept people for who they were and allow conversations about personal stuff. So she felt good about helping support a safe and curious culture at ProcessCorp.

She continued to be curious about Pauline, though. Pauline's personality structure was novel to Kayla, partly because it was so different from hers, and partly because she had negative associations with Promoter energy in her past. She wanted to learn more.

One morning Kayla saw Pauline walking toward the break room, so she followed her.

After some small talk, Kayla initiated, "Pauline, I've been meaning to ask you about something. I'm so curious about the Promoter personality type. It's not very strong in my condo." Using Pauline's preferred Directive channel of communication, Kayla continued, "Tell me how you experience it and how that's been for you here at ProcessCorp."

Pauline lit up. "I will. Promoter is, indeed, my Base. Of course, I have five other floors in my personality just like you. Let me show you." Pauline gestured toward her office.

Kayla followed Pauline to her office. Pauline grabbed the acrylic desk stand holding her personality condo from her desk and showed Kayla. "My Base is Promoter. My next floor is Thinker and that's my current Phase. Then Harmonizer next. After that, my next three floors are pretty small, so it takes a lot of energy for me to appreciate and communicate with those types in others. It's a work in progress.

"But you asked how it's been for me at ProcessCorp," Pauline continued. "PCM has really challenged me. I'm a no-nonsense person. My Promoter Base wants to cut to the chase and just get stuff done. This is where Sam and I have had conflicts in the past."

Kayla interrupted, "But you seem so good at it now. I see how you talk differently to people and seem to practice the Platinum Rule effortlessly."

"Thank you for that, Kayla. I'm glad you notice. It's not easy and it's taken a lot of work. Collecting ROI data was huge for me. That's when things started to click. I'm guessing it struck a chord with my Thinker Phase. It was rational data that supported the hard work we were doing to individualize our communication for each personality type. And, it's not like I'm heartless. My Harmonizer floor is third strongest, and I have about 60 percent energy there. So I can energize my compassionate side when I need to."

Kayla recalled, "I saw that the other day when you reassured Mario when his proposal wasn't chosen."

"Yep, that's right. In that situation I was able to empathize with Mario's loss because we both have a Thinker Phase, so those kinds of situations are particularly difficult for us. I channeled my Harmonizer energy to show compassion and support."

Pauline continued, "I'm not perfect though. It's an ongoing discipline to recognize and honor my unique way of approaching things, and help others do the same. It's both a mindset and a skillset. The mindset is that everyone is valuable, capable, and responsible. It's a decision to keep these switches on every day.[1] The skillset is using the tools of PCM to help that potential come alive in relationships.

I constantly remind myself that PCM is about types *in* people, not types *of* people. Since I have all those same types in me, I try to channel my own energy to connect with others."

"What about you, though? Do you ever feel like you are losing yourself in the process?" Kayla asked.

"Great question, Kayla. I worried about that at first, but here's the deal. You can't change your personality—in other words, the order of your floors—you can only work with it to become more nimble and agile. I have to respect and take care of my personality structure in order to be healthy. If I ignore my Base Promoter's need for action, I can really become a negative influence around here. I get impatient with people and stop supporting them, preferring to just go it alone. That doesn't make me a very good team player. The positive part is that my Promoter is really adaptable, and I love to figure out how to connect with people. It's like a challenge. It's a personal victory for me when others feel heard and motivated in a genuine way.

"If I don't get my Thinker Phase needs for recognition of productive work and time structure met in a healthy way, I attempt to get them met negatively and become a nasty micromanager. That's my Thinker distress behavior. Nobody likes that. Sam and I like to share horror stories from our past of being in Thinker distress. It helps us remember not to go there again."

Kayla expressed what was becoming clear to her. "So it still comes down to taking care of our own personality first?"

"You got it Kayla. You can't see others through until you see yourself through. They go hand in hand."

You can't see others through until you see yourself through first.

Kayla wanted to thank Pauline for opening up and sharing her personal story. But before she opened her mouth, she realized that she was affirming what was important to her, personal connection.

That's not what motivated Pauline. So instead of practicing the Golden Rule, Kayla energized her Thinker floor to offer Pauline's Phase motivational needs. "Pauline, thanks for taking the time to explain this to me. It made a lot of sense and I can really see how much more effective and productive your team is because you practice PCM."

Pauline beamed. "Thank you, Kayla. I'm here for you if you ever want to talk. I can tell you are gonna rock with this PCM stuff."

Kayla realized what had just happened. She smiled all the way back to her desk.

After she sat down, Kayla noticed Mario standing at the copy machine across the office. Her observations of his behavior were consistent with a Thinker Base, and that's what Pauline had told her. Kayla felt energized and recognized that it was because her own needs were getting met positively. So she decided to keep practicing PCM. She went over to Mario and initiated the Requestive (Asking) channel. Temporarily subduing her natural warmth and playful energy, Kayla energized her Thinker floor to adopt a more serious tone and rigid posture. "Mario, what are you working on?"

Mario turned around and replied in a monotone voice, "I am making copies of a proposal for a client meeting this afternoon."

"I guess we are communicating," Kayla told herself. "This is how Requestive channel with Thinkers is supposed to work. I asked him for information and he gave it to me, no emotions involved." She remembered the Rule of Communication from PCM Training: Communication occurs when there is an offer and a response in the same channel. So she continued by initiating the Requestive channel again with Mario. "Pauline invited me to this meeting but I don't know many details. What are the most important details I should know?"

Mario stopped what he was doing, turned around, and gave Kayla his full attention. "As soon as I finish making these copies I have a few free minutes. I'd be happy to give you a quick briefing."

"Sounds great. I'll be at my desk. Will you come get me?" Kayla asked, continuing to use Mario's favorite channel.

"Yes." Mario turned back toward the copy machine.

"It's so clear," Kayla realized as she went back to her desk. "Using someone's favorite channel could really reduce miscommunication and improve efficiency." She remembered another comment her PCM trainer, Sandy, had made: that channels are like mini-contracts between two people. When we use someone's favorite channel and when we reciprocate in the channel that's offered to us, we let people know we can be trusted.

The next day was Kayla and Pauline's weekly ProcessCorp integration session. Pauline was ready to jump right in. "Good morning, Kayla! Great to see you. I enjoyed our last meeting and have been looking forward to continuing the conversation. How are you doing?"

"I'm doing great, Pauline. I have a ton to share with you from my homework assignment."

"Let's get to it." Pauline leaned forward in her chair with curiosity and focus. Kayla was much more aware of Pauline's Promoter Base perception of action.

Kayla told Pauline all about the connections she'd made and how she had applied PCM in her conversations with Lucas and Mario.

POSITIVE VERSUS NEGATIVE INFLUENCE

Pauline inquired, "Kayla, how did you feel when you used different parts of your personality to make a stronger connection with others?"

Kayla thought for a moment, "I felt good. I'm almost afraid to say this, but I felt powerful. In the past when I didn't feel understood or there was miscommunication, I would usually just give in or make excuses. I felt powerless or defensive. Recently, though, I've realized that within me is a lot more potential than I ever imagined. When I can find that energy and use it to respect where someone else is coming from, it's amazing."

"You were afraid to feel powerful?" Pauline asked.

Kayla answered, "Yeah, because the last thing I want to do is manipulate or control people. Yet, when I adjusted how I communicated, I got dramatic results."

Pauline got more serious, "Real connection is powerful. PCM enables much greater influence than most people are used to. And you are right, the last thing we want to do is manipulate or control people. Many leaders abuse psychological tools or personality models. They use the tools to see through people instead of seeing people through. They act like people are some puzzle to figure out so you can get what you want."

Kayla was serious, too. "I want to be a leader who sees people through. How do I know the difference?"

Pauline smiled, "That's what I was hoping to explore with you today. Thanks for bringing it up!

"Influence can be positive or negative. Leadership is about leveraging individual differences toward shared goals. When we are getting our Phase needs met in positive ways and helping others do the same, we can exert positive influence.

Leadership is about leveraging individual differences toward shared goals.

"But we don't always get our needs met in healthy ways. Sometimes we forget to take care of ourselves. Sometimes we encounter stress that makes it really hard to get our needs met. Sometimes we are in situations that are toxic to our needs. Sometimes we are just plain stubborn. We know better and we still don't do it."

"This sounds familiar," Kayla interrupted. "In my last PCM training session I learned about the relationship between positive and negative attention. When we don't get our Phase needs met in positive ways, we will attempt to get those very same needs met negatively, with or without awareness. It's so predictable!"

"Tell me about it!" Pauline reacted. "This is huge. PCM shows us how we can exert positive influence, and how in distress we will exert negative influence by trying to get our needs met negatively."

Kayla clarified, "So you are saying that if I am getting my needs met negatively in distress, then I am exerting negative influence?"

"Yes, Kayla," Pauline responded. "And, to make matters worse, distress invites distress. When I am in distress, I invite others into distress."

"That's crazy. Why does that happen?" Kayla wondered out loud.

SELF-DECEPTION AND THE IRONY OF INTENT

Pauline explained, "There are some things about distress that are as old as human relationships, and incredibly pertinent to leadership. Recognizing these dynamics is critical to staying healthy and seeing people through.

"It starts with recognizing the reality that we are all motivated to meet our Phase needs, consciously or unconsciously. And, like I said earlier, sometimes we don't accomplish it in a healthy way, for whatever reason. Then, we attempt to get those very same needs met negatively. It's not that humans want to sabotage themselves, but in the absence of positive attention, negative attention is second best. Humans would rather have negative attention than none at all."

"People do some pretty icky stuff in distress. How do we live with ourselves?" Kayla's Harmonizer Base was truly curious why people would do mean things on purpose.

"Self-deception and self-justification," Pauline answered. "In distress, we start to deceive ourselves about who's worthwhile and under what conditions. That's how we justify our negative behavior toward ourselves and others. Of course, then we have to get others to buy into the deception so we don't have to be as responsible for our negative behavior. Our behavior is designed to get others hooked so they play along with it. All the while, we can't see the forest for the trees because we are focused on proving our version of reality, not doing what's effective or healthy."

"Our version of reality?" Kayla asked.

Pauline continued, "Yeah, think of it like this: our healthy modus operandi is to get our needs met positively. That's our positive intention. In distress, we deceive ourselves into accepting a different modus operandi, a negative, self-sabotaging intention. PCM predicts exactly what it is and how it hurts us."

"I learned about the distress behaviors of each Phase, but nothing about negative modus operandi. Tell me more," Kayla directed Pauline, staying with Pauline's favorite channel.

"Let's get specific, Kayla, and I'll start with me. Then, we can look at your profile. My Phase is Thinker. My positive needs are recognition of productive work and time structure. When I can arrange for these needs to be met positively, I am a happy camper because I am fulfilling my positive intention. I have more energy and flexibility to ride my elevator to other floors in my condo and practice the Platinum Rule. It's so much easier to see people through.

"However, when I don't get these needs met positively, I do some pretty predictable things. My early warning signs are that I start to believe that I have to be perfect to be worthwhile, so I overthink and overexplain everything. You might notice that my emails get longer and more convoluted because I can't get to the point until I've completely explained myself. I convince myself that I can do it better and faster than anyone else, so I don't delegate. Not very helpful as a leader."

Kayla chuckled to herself. She had been the recipient of such an email from Pauline. She remembered reading it and wondering what the heck Pauline was even trying to say.

Pauline must have noticed. "I know, I know. Isn't it ironic that I think I can do it better and faster myself, but my emails take longer for everyone to read and only confuse people?

"Where things really take a turn for the worse, though, is when I replace my positive modus operandi with my Thinker's negative intention of being in control. When I don't get positive recognition for my work or time structure, I start to control everyone else's work and time structure. I micromanage and get pretty critical, convincing myself that the problem is that other people are lazy, stupid, and wasting time."

"Is that where your and Sam's horror stories come from?" Kayla wondered out loud.

"Yep. And here's the inevitable consequence of my distress behavior: morale plummets and productivity eventually goes down.

Because of me, everybody is running around scared, angry, and second-guessing themselves. The irony of it all is that by choosing my negative modus operandi of control as an alternative to my positive needs, I sacrifice the things that matter most to me, productivity and efficiency. It's like making a deal with the devil where I feel justified at first, but always lose in the long run."[2]

"Wow, that's intense. I guess Karma really is a bitch."

Pauline laughed, "Yep, you got it! And it gets worse."

"How can it get worse?" Now Kayla was laughing.

"Remember the Phase issue, that emotional Achilles's heel that can trip us up when we don't deal with it authentically?"

Kayla thought for a moment, then blurted out the connection she had just made. "Oh my goodness! Grief and loss. That's the Thinker's Achilles's heel. The irony is that the more they try to control things, the more they lose control over the things they value most."

"Exactly," Pauline chimed in. "So we Phase Thinkers in distress keep getting more and more opportunities to experience the grief associated with loss. If we recognize what's happening, we can authentically grieve the losses, recognize that we aren't in control, and start getting our needs met positively again."

"I suppose that's easier said than done, huh?" Kayla suggested.

"Yes, especially since in distress we are invested in self-deception and justification. Sometimes it takes a significant event or outside help to bring us back to reality." Pauline paused reflectively. "And sometimes by the time we figure it out, it's too late to go back to the way things were."

"What do you mean?" Kayla asked.

Pauline's tone was reflective and serious. "When I was in my Promoter Phase I spent a long time in distress, engaging in my negative modus operandi of manipulation and pursuing supremacy by trying to dominate everyone. But I lost my ability to lead others and the glory faded. By the time I took responsibility for my behavior and authentically addressed my Phase issue of bonding and intimacy, there was no going back. I got healthy, which was awesome.

But my new normal wasn't the same. I experienced a Phase change to Thinker, the next floor in my condo. As a result, I had different motivational needs. The old Promoter Phase need for incidence didn't fill my tank in the same way it used to."

Kayla pressed, "How do you know if it's too late to go back?"

"There's no magic test you can take, but there are a few criteria that help us get a pretty good idea. If these three things all happen, there's a good chance that a person will experience a Phase change: they are 1) stuck in negative attention distress behavior most of the time, for at least six months to two years, 2) during that time, they are avoiding dealing authentically with their Phase issue, and 3) they eventually recognize what's happening, take personal responsibility for their situation, and address the Phase issue authentically."

"Some people seem to be in distress their whole lives," Kayla mused. "I wonder if they ever take the third step."

"Yeah, I know people like this. It's really unfortunate because they are miserable and they just keep attracting more drama and misery. But enough about me. Kayla, are you still interested in seeing how the irony of intent plays out with your personality?"

"It's pretty complicated. I don't get it." Kayla's tone was strained and she felt pressure in her chest.

Pauline jumped in with extra energy. "No doubt! This whole irony thing is like getting hit in the face with your own fist. Put up your hand."

Kayla had no idea what Pauline was doing, but she put her hand up. Pauline pulled a small rubber ball out of a basket on her desk and threw it at Kayla's hand. It bounced back at Pauline, knocking over her water glass. A little water spilled on the floor.

Kayla laughed out loud and blurted out, "Okay, what just happened?!"

Pauline had a wry smile on her face. "Just messing around trying to lighten the mood. That was my attempt at offering your Phase need of contact."

Kayla loved how much better she felt, and hated how obvious it was. "Okay, that's PCM voodoo magic," was all that came out.

"Positive influence, Kayla. I noticed you were getting drained from all these logical connections I was asking you to make. So I tried offering you contact as a way to help energize you for the next few minutes of our meeting."

"Well, it worked!" Kayla said, smiling. "Now I'm ready to try analyzing my own stuff."

"Lay it on me!" Pauline replied.

"Well, I just showed you my early warning sign," Kayla began. "I get confused and can't think clearly so I say things like, 'I don't get it.' It's not that I'm stupid, I just can't think clearly so I try to get others to do it for me. My Phase Rebel need is contact. If I can get daily doses of creative activity and move around I'm in a great space. If I don't get contact in a positive way, my distress behavior is to blame others and avoid any responsibility for my own behavior. I get negative contact by complaining and making excuses when people try to get me to apologize or take responsibility."

"Makes sense to me." Pauline could see the logic.

"So what's my negative modus operandi?" Kayla asked rhetorically. "Hmm, I certainly know how to push people's buttons when I'm in distress. I have been accused of that by Lucas."

"You're on to something, here," Pauline affirmed. "The fancy word for it is 'provoke.' Rebel blaming behavior is all about provoking people to get a negative reaction. That makes it easier to blame them for your problems."

"I get it!" Kayla reacted. "It's like I get a jolt of satisfaction when somebody gets upset or yells at me, even though I hate it when people are mad."

"And then what happens?" Pauline probed.

"Usually I get even more pressure to step up, take responsibility, or admit I did it. It really cramps my style. I feel trapped and want to escape."

"Isn't it ironic," Pauline mused. "The more you provoke people, the more they try to control you. There goes your spontaneity and creativity, huh?"

"Yep, it really stinks," Kayla agreed. "And the only way out is to take responsibility for my own feelings and behaviors, own up, and make it right. But that brings me face to face with my Phase issue of responsibility. It's just like you said, getting hit in the face with my own fist."

"The good news is that you recognize it and have tools to get yourself out of it." Pauline's voice was reassuring.

"Feel it, share it, ask for help, solve it with my special set of skills?"

"That's the ticket!" Pauline reacted. "Before we wrap up, I want to connect all this to seeing people through at ProcessCorp.

"When we are in distress, pursuing our negative modus operandi, we'd much rather be justified than do anything effective or healthy. And it's amazing how much energy people will spend to achieve it. It's impossible to see people through when we are in distress because our goal is to justify our own false belief about someone's value, capability, or responsibility rather than influence those positive gifts toward shared goals."

"That sounds draining." Kayla had a flashback to her last job.

"I know, right?!" Pauline responded. "And it infects entire cultures. Toxic cultures spend all their energy trying to control negative behavior and feel justified. They can't get a handle on the problem because they aren't dealing with the root cause."

"Let me guess," Kayla interrupted. "People will attempt to get their needs met negatively as long as they aren't getting them met positively. So focusing on the negative behavior only makes things worse."

"Yes!" Pauline was getting more passionate. "Negative attention is a symptom of the problem. Yet, so many leaders and organizations keep chasing an illusion trying to control the symptoms. More policies, more oversight, more power struggles. It's like if you punished your car when the empty fuel warning light went on. Pure insanity."

"But then again, distress is insanity," Pauline continued after a pause, "because we spend all this energy trying to get negative attention, avoiding our Phase issues, tearing ourselves and each other down, all the while justifying it as okay."

"So what's the solution?" Kayla was more animated.

"The solution is to fill the tank with fuel. Or electricity if that's what your car prefers." Pauline stopped and waited for Kayla to respond.

"Give people what they really need, their Phase motivational needs?" Kayla offered.

"Exactly. This may seem too simple to be so effective, but if someone gets their Phase motivational needs met positively, they don't need to get them met negatively. Only one side of the coin can be facing up at any given time. What this means, Kayla, is that we have a fundamental choice to make when distress happens. Get sucked into the dynamic of justification and self-deception or see people through by meeting our own and others' motivational needs in a positive way."

"Pauline, is what you are saying at all related to the book you have on your desk?" Kayla went to Pauline's desk and picked up a book titled *Leadership and Self-Deception*.[3]

"That's one of my favorite books and has influenced me so much. It really helped me understand some dynamics of distress, especially as a leader. The authors of this book, The Arbinger Institute, have done some phenomenal work on unpacking the attitudes, mindsets, and behaviors that connect people versus alienating and separating. They have so much to offer on seeing people through."

"I need to get a copy," Kayla remarked.

"Would you like to borrow mine?" Pauline offered, then continued, "And with PCM, you can take Arbinger's wisdom to a whole new level. What PCM does that no other framework can do is unpack these dynamics based on individual personality differences and predict exactly how each personality type will behave in distress. And it doesn't stop there. PCM guides you on how to recognize what's happening and intervene positively to turn things around, for any personality structure."

SEEING PEOPLE THROUGH WHEN DISTRESS OCCURS

"This sounds really hard." Kayla recognized she was going into distress again and decided to take responsibility for what she wanted. So she continued, "How do we actually turn things around? What does it take?"

Pauline explained, "This is where it gets real, Kayla. Responding constructively to distress in ourselves or others is really hard because the temptation is to seek justification. It's so much easier than offering people what they really need. Here's a four-step template we use at ProcessCorp.

"The first step is to become intimately aware of your own distress behavior. What types of interactions or situations are most difficult for you? What are your early warning signs? Your PCM Profile gives some general patterns to look for. The more you can fill in the specifics with your own behavior the more helpful this step will be. When you recognize these, it's okay to ask for help. In fact, you'd be surprised how well your friends, family, and coworkers actually know your distress behavior. They probably see it before you do.

"Step two is to develop your repertoire of skills for getting your Phase motivational needs met in healthy ways. Again, your PCM Profile action plan gives some suggestions, but only you know what works best for you. Sometimes you have to get creative. Sometimes you have to set boundaries with people. It's just like healthy diet and exercise.

"Step three is to make friends with your Phase issue. You've made a lot of progress on this already, so you are on your way. The Phase issue is sneaky because it creeps up on you when you are least expecting it. As you develop your comfort and competence with handling it, you'll be much less likely to go into distress.

"Step four is to learn about the other five personality types. This way you can recognize their distress behavior, develop your skills in helping them get their needs met, and support them in dealing openly with their Phase issues."

"It looks like my profile report has a lot of valuable information in it." Kayla was looking forward to reviewing her profile again in light of today's conversation.

Pauline continued, "These four steps are a lifelong process, Kayla. Using PCM to see people through is a way of life and a philosophy of how we are with people, especially as leaders. Working on these steps every day requires a lot of self-awareness and humility. When someone is in your face with their negative attention behavior and inviting you to play the game of distress, it requires a lot of presence and humility to see beyond the bluster, and communicate with the valuable, capable, and responsible person behind that behavior."

"Any homework today?" Kayla asked.

"Yes." Pauline answered, "Let's start with step one, becoming intimately familiar with your distress behavior. I invite you to interview four people this week, two from inside ProcessCorp, and two from your personal life—ideally people who know you pretty well. Show them your profile and describe your Phase needs and distress behavior. Then, ask these people to tell you what they see. The goal is to get an accurate account of your distress behavior. It's not about self-criticism, it's about honest self-assessment. Are you willing to do that this week?"

"I'm willing," Kayla responded. "It doesn't sound fun, but I'm ready to learn all I can about myself so I can see myself through."

RESOURCE GUIDES

Table 7: Positive Motivational Needs for Each Phase Type

Personality Phase Type	Phase Needs*	Details
Thinker	Recognition of productive work	Recognition of productive work means you thrive on achievement. You need to be productive and efficient. Planning and accomplishing tasks is intrinsically rewarding. You enjoy solving problems using your logical thinking skills.
	Time structure	Time structure means you value time and how it is spent. It is important for you to use your time efficiently and productively.
Persister	Recognition of purposeful work	Recognition of purposeful work means knowing you are doing what matters. Your work is a reflection of your values, so you are motivated when you can see evidence that you have contributed to advancing what's most important.
	Conviction	Conviction needs are about respecting your core beliefs and values. This happens each day when you make decisions about what you will and won't do.
Harmonizer	Recognition of person	Recognition of person means you need to know you are unconditionally appreciated for who you are as opposed to what you do. You love serving your team and organization when there's a safe, supportive, and friendly environment.
	Sensory	Sensory needs are about feeding the senses. You recharge by nurturing yourself with things that feel good, smell good, sound good, taste good, and look good.
Rebel	Contact	Contact means interacting with novel and stimulating things in order to get your creativity flowing. Movement, play, and unexpected interactions fuel your brain and give you energy.
Imaginer	Solitude	Solitude is about having unstructured and uninterrupted time to yourself with no expectations. In a crowd, or in a park, you can retreat to a quiet place inside to recharge.
Promoter	Incidence	Incidence involves a lot of action in a short period of time. Risk, excitement, and challenge are energizing.

* PCM Profiles provide extensive detail on specific strategies for meeting Phase needs. To obtain your own PCM Profile, visit SeeingPeopleThrough.com.

Table 8: Environments that Naturally Energize and Challenge Each Phase Type

Personality Type	Energizing Environments	Challenging Environments
Thinker	Situations with clear structure, guidelines, chain of command, feedback, and linear flow	Situations with little structure, unclear chain of command and information flow, lack of feedback, large groups, emotional nuances, instability
Persister	Situations requiring ethical standards, moral authority, visioning the "right course"	Situations with shifting "rules of engagement," gray areas, contradictory data, and emotional nuance
Harmonizer	Sensitive situations with emotional nuance, requiring empathy and compassion	When asked to "be tough," "act like a man," or discouraged from talking about family and emotions or adding a personal touch at work
Rebel	Rapid change, with unpredictable external situations, when creative and flexible solutions are required	Rigid procedures, prescribed discipline, linear project flow, expectations, preaching
Imaginer	Low-stimulation environments, working alone, repetitive tasks, hands-on work	Situations with lots of people and conversation, emotional nuance, rapid-fire discussions, typical meetings
Promoter	Unpredictable fast-paced situations, when stakes are high and resourceful problem-solving is required	Slow pace, deliberate and structured problem-solving, lots of analysis, prescribed procedures, low-risk, emotional nuance

Table 9: Positive Phase Needs, Early Warning Signs, and Negative Attention Distress Behavior

Positive Phase Needs	First Degree Early Warning Signs*	Second Degree Negative Attention Distress*
Recognition of productive work Time structure	**I must be perfect to be worthwhile** You will experience a compulsion to show how perfectly you can think.	**Overcontrolling** You will believe that you are worthwhile and others are not worthwhile because they are lazy, stupid, disorganized, and/or irresponsible. As a result, you will attempt to exert more and more control to make people and things do what you want.
Recognition of purposeful work Conviction	**Others must be perfect to be worthwhile** You will experience a compulsion to correct the imperfections in others.	**Pushing Beliefs** You will believe that you are worthwhile and others are not worthwhile because they lack moral character and don't care enough about what's important. As a result, you will attempt to push your beliefs on people in order to protect them.
Recognition of person Sensory	**I must please you to be worthwhile** You will experience a compulsion to keep the peace at any cost.	**Making Mistakes** You will believe that others are worthwhile, and you are not worthwhile because you are undeserving. As a result, you will lose confidence in yourself and make mistakes that invite criticism from others.
Contact	**I must try hard to be worthwhile** You will experience needing to make extra effort to think clearly.	**Blaming** You will believe that you are worthwhile, and others are not worthwhile because it's their fault, not yours. As a result, you will avoid responsibility for your behavior and feelings.
Solitude	**I must be strong to be worthwhile** You will experience detaching from your thoughts and feelings, as if they aren't part of you.	**Withdrawing** You will believe that others are worthwhile, and you are not worthwhile. You may withdraw, avoid people, and isolate.
Incidence	**Others must be strong to be worthwhile** You will experience an urge to make others more self-sufficient.	**Manipulating** You will believe that you are worthwhile, and others are not worthwhile because they are weak. So you maneuver situations to take advantage of people.

* PCM describes three predictable and observable degrees of distress. The first degree of distress is the early warning sign. Second degree is when people get their needs met negatively. Third degree, characterized by depression and despair, is common for all types and is not listed on this table. PCM Profiles provide extensive detail on specific behaviors characterizing the distress for each type. To obtain your own PCM Profile, go to SeeingPeopleThrough.com.

Table 10: The Irony of Intent

Positive Phase Needs	Negative Phase Needs	Negative Intent (Modus Operandi)	Sacrifices	Intensifies the Phase Issue
Recognition of productive work Time structure	Overcontrolling	Control *The intention is to prevent any unexpected outcomes*	Morale and effectiveness	More **loss** of time and opportunity
Recognition of purposeful work Conviction	Pushing Beliefs	Power *The intention is to command absolute authority*	Respect and integrity	More **fear** of unknown threats
Recognition of person Sensory	Making Mistakes	Martyrdom *The intention is to smother people with help, then get rejected*	Self-esteem	More **angry** about all I've given and being taken advantage of
Contact	Blaming	Provoking *The intention is to get a negative reaction*	Spontaneity	Forced to be **responsible**
Solitude	Withdrawing	Isolation *The intention is to be left alone*	Imagination	No one is coming, only you can exercise **autonomy** to take the next step
Incidence	Manipulating	Supremacy *The intention is to dominate*	Glory	Ultimately, relationships and **bonding** are necessary for success

Each personality Phase type's primary intention is to get positive psychological needs met. In distress they attempt to get those very same needs met negatively. The self-justified modus operandi is an unconscious negative intention that leads inevitably into failure by reinforcing self-sabotaging sacrifices. As a result, the Phase issue is presented even more intensely.

Table 11: Steps for Seeing People Through When Distress Occurs

Step	Skills to Develop	Self-reflection Questions
1. Know your own distress	Recognize situations and interactions that invite you into distress. Become intimately aware of your typical distress behaviors.	• What situations require character strengths that are least developed in my personality? How do I respond? • When and where am I exposed to challenging environments? (See Table 8.) • What are my Phase (and Base) warning signs and negative attention behaviors? (See Table 9 and your personal PCM Profile.) • What do my peers, employees, and friends see when I am in distress?
2. Meet your needs	Recognize your Phase (and Base, if different) motivational needs. Develop habits and skills for meeting your needs in healthy ways every day.	• What are my Phase (and Base) motivational needs? (See Table 7 and your personal PCM Profile.) • How will I respond to distress by arranging to get my needs met positively? Who will I ask for help? • How will I proactively meet my needs positively every day? Who will I ask for help?
3. Recognize distress in others	Recognize situations and interactions that invite others into distress. Become intimately aware of others' typical distress behaviors.	• What situations require character strengths that are least developed in my employees, peers, family? How do they respond? • When and where are they exposed to challenging environments? (See Table 8.) • What are their Phase (and Base) warning signs and negative attention behaviors? (See Table 9. Ask to see their personal PCM Profiles.) • What do I see when they are in distress?
4. Feed others' needs	Recognize others' Phase (and Base, if different) motivational needs. Develop habits and skills for meeting others' needs in healthy ways every day.	• What are the Phase (and Base) motivational needs of my peers, employees, family? (See Table 7. Ask to see their PCM Profiles.) • How will I respond to their distress by offering their positive needs? • How will I proactively offer their positive needs every day?

Use the self-reflection questions in this table to guide your response when distress occurs. Apply these steps in order. Leaders cannot recognize and respond positively to others' needs when they are in distress, so steps 1 and 2 are always a priority. Refine as needed.

SIX

Trust

Earn trust, earn trust, earn trust. Then you can worry about the rest.

—Seth Godin

There is no universal definition of trust, and it's a mistake to assume that because you are trustworthy according to your own definition, people should or will trust you. Trust should never be assumed and must be earned in every interaction. That's easier said than done because trust has different meanings for different people.

Trust is influenced in large part by our personality. People who speak the same language, share the same character strengths, and are motivated the same way tend to seem more trustworthy to us. We understand each other and know what to expect.

Earning trust and being trustworthy requires leaders to move beyond their own definitions and implement personality-specific behaviors depending on who they are interacting with. The Platinum Rule applies to trust as well. Earn trust from others as they want to be trusted.

We've polled thousands of people on their definition of trust. Over and over, it boils down to one of two questions:

Am I safe with you?
Can I count on you?

Answering these questions positively in every interaction builds trust. PCM offers even more specific guidance on how leaders can build trust by interacting with a person's favorite channel and Perception, offering their Phase and Base motivational needs, and supporting them in dealing authentically with their Phase issue.

Resource guides at the end of this chapter show how to recognize early signs of communication breakdown and how to build trust with each type.

———————

Two things surprised Kayla about her homework. The first was how difficult it was to tell people about her distress behavior. She felt vulnerable and exposed. The second surprise was how open people were with her about it. They didn't seem nearly as nervous about it as she did. Lucas's feedback was pretty predictable since they'd talked about it before. He explained that in distress Kayla would often "play dumb" at first, as if she didn't understand. If Lucas got hooked and started asking more complicated questions, Kayla would make excuses and complain. That's when the arguments would start.

Kayla's profile included distress patterns for both her Base Harmonizer floor, and her Phase Rebel floor. PCM training taught Kayla that after a person has experienced a Phase change, the motivators and corresponding distress of his/her Base floor are still important but are secondary.

Kayla called her dad to ask about distress growing up, when Kayla had been in a Harmonizer Phase. Her dad recalled that she would get tentative and worry about pleasing everyone, often followed by putting herself down. Her dad also described how Kayla seemed to pick the worst time to interrupt his band practice and that's when he would get angry and tell her to leave. Kayla wondered if that was what her profile report called making mistakes: inadvertently behaving in a way that invites criticism and rejection instead of positive acceptance. It reminded her of the irony of intent conversation with Pauline.

Kayla wanted Pauline's input because she felt they had a good connection and Pauline was her department supervisor. Pauline had been very supportive and open to conversation in previous interactions. Remembering that Pauline was in a Thinker Phase and respecting her time structure, Kayla asked Pauline for a time on her schedule that might work. Pauline was happy to help and had an opening that afternoon.

After Kayla described her profile and distress behaviors, she asked Pauline, "So what behavior do you see in me when I am in distress?"

"Kayla, I'm so glad you asked," Pauline began. "I was hoping you would include me in your homework, especially since we work so closely together. Honestly, I don't experience you in distress very much, and I hope this means you are getting your needs met here at ProcessCorp."

"I am, for sure!" Kayla replied. "I was just telling Mario about how much I appreciate the freedom to move around, and the positive energy around the department."

Pauline seemed pleased. "That's terrific, Kayla. We make an effort to offer everyone the type of communication and environment that fills their tank while also respecting our own needs so we can all function at our best."

WHO'S DRIVING YOU?

Pauline continued, "Before I share specifics, I want to reassure you that distress is a normal part of life. Every one of us dips in and out of distress many times a day. The question isn't whether or not we are in distress, but how quickly we recover. Distress is only a problem when we are getting negative attention day after day without recovering. That's when our behavior really starts to infect relationships and culture. That's why it's so important that we recognize our own distress and have effective strategies to get out as quickly as possible; and help others do the same. Did you learn about how Dr. Terry McGuire used PCM at NASA?"

"Yeah, and it was fascinating," Kayla recalled. "He used PCM to help NASA select and train astronauts for the space shuttle program. I guess when you are sending a small group of America's best pilots into space, you want to know they can get along and function at their best. You can't replace a distressed astronaut with a healthy one just because they are having a bad day."

"That's what seeing people through is all about. Each astronaut had to be a leader, incredibly self-aware and self-managed, and be able to support the others in doing the same. PCM helped them do that. Thankfully, we aren't operating the space shuttle, but our mission matters to us and our customers, and that's the most important thing." Pauline beamed with pride.

"Okay, back to your distress. The most common things I see come from both your Harmonizer Base and your Rebel Phase. I notice that sometimes when you aren't sure about where you fit on the team or in a project, which is totally understandable at this point, you get quiet and lose assertiveness. When people ask you what you want, you don't answer directly. You say things like, 'Whatever you want is fine with me.'

"I'm pretty sure you know what you want. I've seen your passion. So when you avoid saying it, I'm guessing you are worrying about being rejected and choose to please people and accommodate rather than speak up. Does this fit, Kayla?"

Kayla felt embarrassed and exposed and wanted to be invisible. Pauline had identified Kayla's Driver, a term used in PCM to indicate the very subtle changes in words, tones, gesture, postures, and facial expressions that indicate a person is moving into distress. Pauline must have noticed because she offered reassurance but didn't avoid the issue. "It's normal to feel uncomfortable, that's okay. Everyone has their own distress and we show it many times a day. I accept you the way you are. I'm curious if you see what I'm seeing."

"Yes," Kayla agreed. "I get what you are talking about. It's my Please You Driver, the one associated with my Harmonizer Base. I feel it. It's like I feel compelled to give in and do whatever I need to do to keep people happy, no matter what I really want."

"I hear you, Kayla. You aren't alone. Every type has their own Driver, and it literally drives our behavior like a car that's been hijacked. Previously I talked about early warning signs. Now you know that PCM calls these early warning signs Drivers. Think back to a specific situation here at work. Do you notice how when you show Driver behavior, someone will usually give you permission to ask for what you want or tell you that it's okay to follow your gut?"

"Yes!" Kayla recalled several situations where she popped right back out of distress when teammates offered her positive affirmation and she immediately felt more confident and shared what she really wanted.

"We don't always catch these second-by-second subtle behavior changes, but we do our best. The cool thing is that you can also interrupt the pattern by giving yourself positive affirmation. You wouldn't believe all the internal self-talk going on around this place!" Pauline laughed as she pointed a finger at her own head and heart.

"What about my Rebel Phase distress behavior. Anything there?" Kayla trusted Pauline more and wasn't afraid to hear her observations.

"Actually, I see less Rebel distress than what I just described from your Base." Pauline began. "This may seem contrary to what you've learned about distress being related to our current Phase floor. Here's why. People will most likely show the Driver of their Base when they encounter stress. This is normal and simply a sign that they are experiencing stress. No problems if it doesn't continue or progress. It's a great indicator that we need to step back, identify what's going on with us, and ask for what we want.

"Phase-specific distress behavior, on the other hand, occurs when we aren't getting our Phase motivational needs met in healthy ways. Phase distress behavior is full-on negative attention, like a white flag being raised, telling ourselves and the world that our gas tank is empty.

"So on any given day, most people will show the Driver behavior of their Base under normal stress, and can easily show the negative attention Phase distress behavior when they aren't getting their Phase needs met positively."

"Wow, that's pretty specific, Pauline." Kayla was intrigued. "This is way more precise and predictive than the other personality model I learned about."

"This is one more reason we like PCM so much," Pauline continued. "Most other models of personality don't distinguish positive and negative attention, or with this much precision on what to look for and how to respond.

"When it comes to your Rebel Phase distress, I most often see you acting confused and making random statements like, 'I don't get it,' or 'This is hard.' Then you stop. You don't say anything else. It's like you are waiting and hoping for someone to jump in and give you the answer or save you from having to experience your own discomfort."

"That's me exactly!" Kayla reacted. "That's my Rebel Try Hard Driver. I'm realizing that I do this when I start to have uncomfortable feelings and I don't like it. When I'm quiet and look confused, I'm wishing for someone else to take over the thinking for me, then I don't have to be responsible for my feelings or actions."

"Wow, that's terrific insight Kayla." Pauline seemed excited. "The Try Hard Driver looks like you are trying hard but can't quite get it. It's a powerful invitation for others to engage negatively in ways that don't support your own value, capability, and responsibility. As they say, distress invites distress."

"I get it! And I can respond positively to Try Hard by relaxing, bringing back the fun, taking ownership over my feelings, and asking for what I need." Instead of feeling exposed, Kayla now felt empowered. She was combining self-awareness with real tools to turn distress around and keep her interactions positive.

Kayla sought out Mario as the second work peer to give feedback. His observations were more analytic, which was no surprise to Kayla given his Thinker Base and Phase. He described how sometimes Kayla would get up from her desk and start walking somewhere, but then turn around and sit back down. This happened on average two to three times a day according to Mario's calculations. Kayla knew exactly what was happening. She often had questions and knew who could help, but would lose confidence once she got up, worrying that she would be perceived as stupid or naive. So she would try hard to figure it out herself.

TRUST IS THE FOUNDATION

At her next integration meeting with Pauline, Kayla shared all about what she'd learned from her interviews and how much safer she felt with her team as time went on. "I'm starting to trust them, and I can tell they trust each other. It's not something I've experienced at other jobs."

"That's wonderful, Kayla. Trust is one of the most important features of a strong culture. Seeing people through is grounded in trust. Another one of my favorite authors, Patrick Lencioni, wrote a book called *The Five Dysfunctions of a Team*.[1] His research showed that the best teams overcome five dysfunctions, the first one being a lack of trust. Without trust, teams can't engage in healthy conflict, they can't hold each other accountable in a safe way, and they can't stay focused on what's most important."

"I totally agree with that," Kayla jumped in. "I wonder if one reason I have shown my Harmonizer Please You Driver a lot here at ProcessCorp is that I'm not sure whether I can trust people. I need to feel safe before I can open up."

"Absolutely," Pauline continued. "Here's something I discovered a while back that never made sense until I learned about PCM. Trust has different meanings to different people. There's no one universal definition of trust. People talk about trust and say they want trust, but they don't realize they have different definitions of what trust actually looks like and feels like. Let's take you for example. You just told me that you need to feel safe in order to open up. That says a lot about your definition of trust."

"That's so true. I need to know that people will accept me and like me the way I am before I really show my cards. If I feel judged, I don't trust someone." Kayla remembered her first boss who always seemed to judge her for not being perfect enough. She hypothesized this to be his You Be Perfect Driver, coming from his Persister Base.

Pauline continued, "What I've realized, Kayla, is that our definition of trust is influenced in large part by our personality. People who have the same perceptual filter, share the same character strengths, and are motivated the same way tend to seem more trustworthy to us.

It's like we just *get* each other and know what to expect. My Phase is Thinker, so I will more likely trust people who think logically and give me the data I need to make decisions. I might struggle to trust someone who is always playing around because I can't count on them to give me what I need in a rational and timely manner. If I am motivated by playful contact like you, I will more likely trust people who are willing to keep it casual with me and accept me the way I am at face value, no strings attached. I might struggle to trust people who are always sharing opinions and judgments."

Kayla noticed a common thread. "So the Platinum Rule applies here as well? Earn trust from others as they want to be trusted."

"Exactly. If I want someone to trust me, then I need to show them the behaviors that matter to them." Pauline leaned back in her chair. "This has been one of the most difficult lessons for me to learn. For a long time here at ProcessCorp I tried to earn trust by doing what I would want from my Thinker Phase, focusing on schedules, task lists, and agendas. This drove the Persister Phase people crazy. They wanted principles, policies, and values. My version of trust actually sent the message that they couldn't count on me to give them what they needed to feel productive and motivated. Not to mention all the Harmonizer Phase people, including Sam, who experience me as bossy and impersonal. She didn't feel safe with me. By practicing the Golden Rule, I became less trustworthy."

"That's so ironic!" Kayla chuckled. "We are all working so hard to be trustworthy in our own way that we miss what others are really looking for. That seems kinda selfish."

Pauline agreed. "I'm with you. I wouldn't go so far as to call it selfish, but I would call it self-focused, or limiting. When we focus instead on seeing people through, we visit other parts of our personality and ask ourselves, 'How can I show this other personality type that they can trust me?'"

WHAT IS YOUR TRUST QUESTION?

"Even if you aren't proficient in all six personality types within you, it boils down to two basic perspectives on trust," Pauline explained. "One perspective defines trust with the question, 'Am I safe with you?' These people define trust as emotional, physical, psychological, and spiritual safety. They need to know they will be valued for who they are, no strings attached.

"The second perspective on trust asks the question, 'Can I count on you?' These people need to know you will do what you say, finish what you start, and follow through on promises. They use words like dependability, integrity, and responsibility to describe trust. Feelings aren't that relevant for this second group."

"I can really see how these two definitions could come into conflict." Kayla realized that this was at the core of her and Lucas's conflicts. "When two people have different definitions of trust, they can do their individual best, but it doesn't work. I can create the most compassionate, safe emotional space for Lucas to show me his real self, but what he really cares about is whether I follow through on my commitments."

What's Your Trust Question?

Am I safe with you?
Can I count on you?

"With PCM, we have a great tool to individualize our behaviors so that we earn trust with all personality types." Pauline was passionate. "That doesn't mean we abandon our own trust definition. Because of our unique personality structure and motivational needs, we have to live out our own version of trust in order to keep our tank filled and stay healthy. You can be a nonjudgmental supportive person for Lucas, because that's who you are. And you can show him you are trustworthy by following through on your promises.

"This is why here at ProcessCorp we learn about each other's trust behaviors and talk openly about it. Along the way we gain a lot more tolerance and appreciation for diversity. But we don't stop there. Seeing people through means acting on what we know. It means actively earning trust by communication with people in the way they prefer. This is how we include and maximize the contribution of all personality types."

Kayla had an idea for a homework assignment. "Pauline, I don't know what you have in mind for me this week, but there's something I'd like to try. May I share it with you?"

"Sure, Kayla. What is it?"

"Last time I interviewed people about my distress behaviors. This time I'd like to interview people about their trust question and figure out how it relates to their personality. What do you think?"

"I love it! That sounds like a great homework assignment. I have nothing to add. I'm excited to hear what you learn." Pauline looked Kayla in the eye and spoke sincerely with a warm tone. "I'm really enjoying getting to know you, Kayla. I appreciate your openness and enthusiasm. It seems like you are buying into our philosophy. Awesome stuff! And by the way, it's okay to do your homework while you are at work. This is part of your job so it's okay to make time for it."

"Thanks! I love this stuff. See you next week!" Kayla already knew one person she wanted to interview. Would she be able to track him down? Would he remember her?

RESOURCE GUIDES

Table 12: Driver, Examples, and Self-affirmations for Each Personality Type

Personality Type	Driver (Belief)	Examples	Self-affirmations
Thinker	Be Perfect	Overexplaining and overdetailing. *"What I meant to say, considering the options, is . . ."* *"Here's a list and three attachments."* *"I've put together a spreadsheet to review our options."*	• I am smart and I can think clearly. • When I stop talking, I won't lose control. Instead, I will gain the opportunity to learn what people really want to know. • Instead of being the expert, I can be a resource.
Persister	You Be Perfect	Asking complicated, rhetorical questions and pointing out what's wrong. *"Do you really think that was the best approach?"* *"I noticed you missed a spot."* *"Don't you believe we should call her first?"*	• I am dedicated and committed. • If I pay more attention to what's working, I'll get more of it. • If I'm a role model instead of a judge, I will have a greater impact.
Harmonizer	Please You	Becoming tentative. *"If it's okay, could we maybe turn down the music?"* *"I'm fine with whatever anyone else wants to do."* *"I guess, if you don't mind."*	• I am a caring, valuable person. • My needs and feelings matter just as much as everyone else. How people respond to me doesn't define me. • I can be a cheerleader instead of a peacekeeper.
Rebel	Try Hard	Can't think or articulate clearly. *"What? I don't get it."* *"Huh? This is hard."* *"What were we supposed to do?"*	• I am a creative person who can think clearly. • It's okay to ask for what I want and seek clarity. • I can use my creativity to find a solution and follow through.
Imaginer	Be Strong	Experiencing detachment from own thoughts and feelings. *"It occurred to me that . . ."* *"One wonders . . ."* *"It seems scary."*	• I am an imaginative person who can think clearly. • It's okay to tell others what's in my head. • It's okay to ask for time and space to reflect.
Promoter	You Be Strong	Expecting others to fend for themselves and toughen up. *"That's what happens when you wait too long."* *"If you can't hunt with the big dogs, stay on the porch."* *"You got this, right?"*	• I am a person of action who can make things happen for others. • Transparency takes bravery, and I can do this! • I can get more done by bringing others alongside me.

Table 13: Trust Question and Trust-building Tips for Each Phase Type

Personality Phase Type	Trust Question	Trust-building Tips
Thinker	Can I count on you?	• Provide them with plenty of data, time frames, and an outline of what you plan to do. • Follow through on what you say you will do, and keep them apprised of pertinent information. • Execute important steps in a timely manner.
Persister	Can I count on you?	• Ask for their opinions, hear their vision and share yours. • Demonstrate your loyalty to the bigger picture. • Follow through on your promises and commitments.
Harmonizer	Am I safe with you?	• Listen to their feelings, show you care about them as a person. • Avoid judgment. • Show them you like them for who they are and will support them emotionally, even when there is pushback.
Rebel	Am I safe with you?	• Be open to new ideas, encourage trial and error. • Avoid micromanaging or preaching at them about what they should or shouldn't do. • Accept them the way they are and give them an open space to experiment and create.
Imaginer	Can I count on you?	• Use explicit commands to elicit their imagination, for example, "Tell me what's on your mind." • Tell them exactly what you want them to do, then leave them alone to do it. • Give them the space and time to imagine new possibilities. • Don't expect them to socialize and brainstorm.
Promoter	Can I count on you?	• Cut to the chase and focus on immediate action. • Give them exciting, time-sensitive, mission-critical tasks. • Keep things moving and avoid getting bogged down in details.

SEVEN

Agility

Stay committed to your decisions, but stay flexible in your approach.

—Tony Robbins

Personality agility is the ability to energize all six types in us. This allows leaders to respect the uniqueness in others and adapt their approach to maximize the people they lead. Agile leaders recognize that no type is better or worse, smarter or less smart. Each one has unique purpose and value. Each one is capable of contributing. Each one is responsible for their choices and behaviors.

Personality diversity is not an obstacle to be overcome. It is an opportunity to see more, be more, and do more. This potential can be realized by using the tools and skills of PCM.

Agility helps the Thinker in us find the most effective method to help each personality type be productive.

Agility helps the Persister in us respect and honor each person according to how they are built.

Agility helps the Harmonizer in us care for and affirm people for who they are, no strings attached.

Agility helps the Rebel in us stay flexible and creative in our leadership.

Agility helps the Imaginer in us realize the endless possibilities of diversity.

Agility helps the Promoter in us quickly get to what works best.

Agile leaders keep their focus on the most important goals and purpose while adjusting their approach depending on the personality of the people they lead.

As soon as Kayla got back to her desk she searched LinkedIn for Mr. Fredricks, her fifth-grade math teacher. She found him! He was still teaching math but had moved from Texas to Oklahoma and was now teaching at the high school level. Kayla sent this message, asking to connect with Mr. Fredricks on LinkedIn: "Greetings Mr. Fredricks. I don't know if you remember me, but you taught my fifth-grade math class at Roosevelt Elementary in Dallas. It was almost 15 years ago. I'm doing an assignment for my new job and would like to interview you."

OLD STUFF. NEW LENS.

Four days later Kayla got a response. Mr. Fredricks accepted Kayla's invitation and sent a message. "Hi Kayla, I'm sorry I don't remember you. It's been a long time. I'm happy to be interviewed though. I'm available most afternoons between 4–5 p.m. Would that work for you? My email and phone number are in my profile information if you want to connect with me that way." Kayla and Mr. Fredricks set up an appointment for the next afternoon.

Kayla was nervous for the call since she had mostly negative memories of Mr. Fredricks. For some reason though, she felt drawn to talk to him. Since learning about PCM, Kayla was truly curious about how personality was involved in some of her most significant relationships growing up. The best-case scenario, she figured, was that she would gain appreciation for his personality and let go of some old baggage. Worst-case scenario is that he'd act the same and she would feel hurt and insignificant again.

Mr. Fredricks picked up the phone. "Hello, this is Chris Fredricks. Is this Kayla?"

"Yes," Kayla responded. "This is Kayla. Thank you for accepting my invite for an interview. It's been a long time and it looks like you've moved and changed to high school math."

"Yeah. I made the shift about five years ago. And, you can call me Chris." Chris continued, "I got married and my wife is a high school teacher. She got a great job offer in Oklahoma, closer to her family, so we moved. The only opening I could find was in high school, so I gave it a try. It's been a good fit for me."

"That's great. I'm happy for you." Kayla felt unexpectedly comfortable. "So, I have a new job, too. My degree is in marketing and I am working at ProcessCorp now. I just started a month ago."

"I've heard about ProcessCorp," Chris interrupted. "They are known for being one of the best places to work in Texas. How do you like it?"

"I love it! I was pretty miserable in my previous jobs and didn't even imagine a place like this could exist. The reason I reached out to you actually has to do with integrating into my new job here. I've been mentoring with my department head and we've been talking about trust. I am supposed to interview people about how they define trust. Can I ask you a few questions?"

"Sure, go ahead." Chris seemed open to the question.

"Well, let's start with your definition of trust," Kayla waited.

"Hmm, let's see. That's an interesting question. How do I define trust?" Chris was silent for a few seconds. "I'd say that trust has to do with integrity and character. I try to walk the talk and I expect others to do the same."

"Interesting. Would you describe some examples of what you mean?" Kayla inquired.

"Sure. When I got married, I told my wife that I'd love her for better or worse. So if I'm having a bad day that's not an excuse for me to love her any less. I made a commitment and I follow through on it. I expect the same from my students. I have high standards and I ask a lot of them. When I say the assignment is due Friday, I mean it."

Kayla was feeling a little anxious now. It seemed like Mr. Fredricks subscribed to a different trust question than Kayla, but she continued. "Mr. Fredricks—I mean Chris—if you don't mind, could you tell me if this definition of trust has changed at all for you over the years?" Immediately Kayla recognized her Harmonizer Please You Driver. She was tentative and lost assertiveness temporarily. While Chris was contemplating his answer, Kayla gave herself a quick pep talk. "It's okay for me to ask these questions. Mr. Fredricks agreed to be interviewed and this assignment is important to me."

Before Chris spoke, Kayla jumped in, "Chris, let me ask that again. Have you always defined trust this way?" She felt much better after asserting herself.

"Yes and no," Chris responded. "I didn't used to care so much about integrity and character. Earlier in my career, probably when I taught you, I would have defined trust as being dependable and competent. I trusted teachers who were on top of their subject and knew their stuff. I didn't trust the touchy-feely ones who only seemed to care about making sure students were happy. I would spend a lot of time preparing for class because I wanted students to trust my knowledge and competence. I wanted them to be able to depend on me to know my stuff. I wanted parents to trust me to instruct their children correctly."

Kayla noticed herself forming a hypothesis about Chris's personality structure. Probably more Persister energy now, more Thinker energy previously in his life. She decided to stay curious.

"So what changed?" Kayla probed, this time with more confidence.

"I'm not sure. I do remember one significant moment during a parent-teacher conference back at Roosevelt. I was explaining to a dad why his daughter was almost failing my class. I described that she didn't speak up and ask questions. When I offered to help during class, she wouldn't say anything. When I'd ask her probing questions to try and get her to figure it out on her own, she would shut down. She made silly mistakes on homework and tests, like she wasn't thinking. I knew that she understood the material better than that. I was quite critical of this student, right in front of her."

Kayla felt a strange sensation coming over her. It was like déjà vu. Surely he wasn't talking about her. There must have been other Harmonizer Phase students in his class. He would have remembered her, wouldn't he?

Chris continued, "I'll never forget what her dad did next. He asked his daughter to leave the room and give us some privacy. Then he told me that his daughter was afraid of me. He explained that she didn't feel safe speaking up because I was asking all these questions and she couldn't think clearly. He explained that his daughter had gotten top grades in math class the year before and that the teacher was supportive and compassionate.

"I remember feeling really angry and wanting to lash out at this dad for the negative comparison. Teachers hate that. But I held my tongue. I said something about just wanting his daughter to be successful, but I didn't really acknowledge what he'd said. It stuck with me though."

"Oh my gosh!" Kayla reacted inside. "That was my dad!" Kayla didn't recall any of the details of that particular parent-teacher conference, but she did remember being asked to leave the room and feeling rejected. She never had the courage to ask her dad about it and he never said anything afterward. Kayla felt ambivalent. Should she reveal the connection, or let it go? She noticed a small amount of compassion for Mr. Fredricks.

Kayla gathered her thoughts. "That must have been hard, Chris. Did that influence your definition of trust?"

"Yes it did," Chris responded. "I reflected a lot on that situation. I wondered if that girl's dad was right. I didn't want students to be afraid of me. I wanted them to love math. My wife also influenced me a lot. She's really good at connecting with students and adjusting how she communicates with each one so that they can hear what she's saying in a way that they can understand. She's always telling me, 'You can't unlock a lock with a lock. You have to unlock a lock with a key.' She says that unless students trust you, they can't really give the energy needed to learn. You've got to find that key that unlocks their energy."

You can't unlock a lock with a lock.
You have to unlock a lock with a key.

"That's the same thing my new boss has been saying!" Kayla felt a connection. "She says that trust comes in different flavors and in order for people to trust us, we have to find that key that fits their definition of trust."

"This is why my definition of trust has changed. I now believe that if I care about students and I want them to learn, then I have to walk the talk. I can't be satisfied with doing my thing in my own way and expect them to learn. It's not one size fits all. If I know this and don't do anything about it, I'm a hypocrite."

Kayla didn't know what to say. She wondered if Mr. Fredricks was now in a Persister Phase. He also seemed to be showing a lot of Harmonizer energy. She wanted to ask so many more questions, but that was beyond her current assignment and there was still the secret she was holding back.

"Kayla, if I could go back in time, I would apologize to that student and her dad. I would tell them I'm sorry for being so rigid in my approach and not realizing how unsafe she felt. I've made a lot of changes in my teaching style and one of them is to be more supportive and compassionate. I've gotten much more flexible. I bet this girl wasn't the only student who felt that way. I probably pushed her away from loving math and I am sorry for that."

Kayla's eyes filled with tears and she felt a lump in her throat. She took a deep breath trying to gather herself and tried to hold back her emotion. But Mr. Fredricks must have noticed. "Are you alright, Kayla?" he asked. "Is it something I said?"

She couldn't hold it in any longer. Through the tears and lump in her throat Kayla shared her secret. "That girl was me, Chris. Honestly, it was not my intention for this to happen and I didn't remember that situation until you described it. My dad never told me about your conversation."

"Oh my goodness, Kayla. I don't know what to say. I feel embarrassed. I am so sorry." Mr. Fredricks was silent.

"It's okay, Chris. You said everything I needed to hear. I accept your apology and I'm so grateful for this unexpected turn of events." Kayla felt like a huge weight had been lifted. She was smiling through the tears.

Kayla and Chris spent the next 15 minutes talking about how their lives had changed and how much they appreciated positive influences in their lives. Kayla told Chris about PCM. While they were on the phone, Chris searched the internet for PCM in education and found a couple of books that had been published on the topic. He was excited to order one and learn more.

Kayla couldn't wait to call her dad, which she did on her way home. She told him the story and they both had a good cry as they replayed that experience and talked about their relationship growing up. Kayla's dad asked if she wanted to come over this weekend for dinner and they could talk more about what she was learning. She was so excited!

PERSONALITY AGILITY

Kayla was eager to tell Pauline. At their next meeting, she spent over half their time sharing what had happened, oblivious to what Pauline may have wanted to talk about. Pauline didn't mind. Things were going just where they needed to go.

"I've been talking nonstop and completely lost track of the time," Kayla apologized.

"Not a problem at all. I love hearing about the breakthroughs and connections you are making. It's amazing how you can go back and rebuild relationships through the lens of PCM. I did that with my dad just before he died. We didn't have the best relationship growing up. He had been diagnosed with prostate cancer and managed to keep things under control for six years going from treatment to treatment. The time came when he recognized that it was a losing battle and continuing to fight it only made his quality of life more miserable.

"My dad's mind was still sharp, so we decided that it was more important that we spend our precious time together strengthening our relationship. That meant tying up loose ends and dealing with unfinished business. That was six years ago, just when I was really getting into PCM. I spent a whole weekend with my parents revisiting some of the pivotal times in our relationship through the lens of PCM. It was so amazing to see things differently and have more appreciation for how hard we tried even when we were totally missing each other's motivational needs. We affirmed our unique personalities and made amends. My dad passed away six months later. I am so grateful for that time we had and the gift of PCM."

"Wow, Pauline. That's a powerful story. I feel more hopeful about strengthening a lot of relationships in my life."

"Over the last few weeks we've learned a lot about how a better understanding of personality helps us see more, do more, and be more." Pauline went over to the whiteboard and wrote in all capital letters the word AGILITY.

"How do you understand this word, Kayla?" Pauline asked.

Kayla's immediate reaction was, "Flexibility, right?"

"Yes, and what else?"

Kayla thought for a moment. She remembered some dog agility videos she watched the other night while scanning social media. She also remembered Mr. Fredricks saying that he had become more flexible with students. "What did those have in common?" Kayla wondered.

"I guess it's more than just flexibility. There's more intention to it. Agility includes deftness, like a border collie negotiating an obstacle course. It's remarkable how they move through it, approaching each challenge with just the right set of skills. Or like Mr. Fredricks, my old math teacher. Now he intentionally adjusts his style to meet students where they are at and this requires a lot of skill and commitment, not just flexibility."

"I love where you're going with this!" Pauline said enthusiastically. "If personality is like an obstacle course, agility is being able to negotiate all six types within us and within others, and to do it deftly, to use your word."

"I get it," Kayla replied, "but I don't like thinking of personality as an obstacle, as something getting in our way. I used to see it that way, but now I see each personality type as a huge opportunity with so much potential. If I'm a border collie, I become one with the course like a masterful dancer!"

Pauline went with the metaphor. "The obstacles aren't there to trip you up. They are there to bring out your best. They aren't separate from you, they are part of the dance, right?"

"Yes! Seeing people through is what happens when we view personality as our partner in the dance of life. It's in us. It's around us. And when we know how to leverage it, it brings out the best in everyone."

"Do you think dogs have personalities?" Kayla couldn't resist the tangent.

"Absolutely! You should talk to Mario. He has a list going of different dog breeds and their unique PCM personalities. It's pretty cool."

Pauline brought their conversation back to the topic. "There's another thing about personality agility to keep in mind. It requires a lot of respect and humility. If you get arrogant and think you've got it all figured out, it's easy to miss something and crash. The most agile leaders I know have a lot of respect for each type in them and honor those differences in others as well."

Kayla checked her understanding, "So a key ingredient for developing personality agility is true respect for the value of each type within us. No type is better or worse, smarter or less smart. Each one has unique purpose and value. Each one is capable of contributing. Each one is responsible."

"Yes, that foundational mindset is critical. When we use the skills of PCM, we can make that mindset a reality through how we treat each other. I'm so excited to see what you do with the communication tools you are learning." Pauline seemed genuinely excited for Kayla.

"Me too!" Kayla agreed. "I am excited to learn all the details about each type and get specific strategies to develop my agility."

"For your homework I want you to think about this one question." Pauline explained, "We know that agility requires that we ride our elevator to different floors of our personality so we can access the qualities and perspective of that type within us. The question is, how do you make sure your elevator is running smoothly? How do you gain access to all these types in you? Going back to the dog agility metaphor, how do you make sure your dog shows up fit and ready to do their best? Will you play with these questions this week?"

"Got it. Will do, Pauline." Kayla was exhausted from the emotional and mental work she'd done in the past week but felt happy and satisfied.

EIGHT

Self-Fullness

In case there is a loss in cabin pressure, yellow oxygen masks will deploy from the ceiling compartment located above you. Please secure your own mask before assisting others around you.

—Preflight safety briefing

Servant leadership is about focusing on serving others and the greater good, keeping our ego out of the equation. This is only possible when leaders are healthy and motivated. When leaders are in distress and attempting to get their needs met in negative ways, they are doing more harm than good. However noble it may seem to put others' needs and interests first, it becomes selfish and destructive when we do it at the expense of our own health. The irony of intent demonstrates that when we deny our own needs, we will inevitably begin operating in ego-based, selfish, and destructive ways.

There's nothing noble or humble about denying our own motivational needs. Leaders who do this chronically soothe their own guilt, avoid conflict, and keep the peace instead of doing the courageous work of setting boundaries and choosing priorities to keep themselves healthy.

Being a self-full leader means taking elegant care of our motivational needs so that we can show up ready to be our best and do our best. It means filling our own tank before we try to serve others.

Only when we meet our own needs first can we energize ourselves to connect more authentically with others.

Leaders are role models and guides. That means we must also support people taking the necessary steps to be self-full. The more we ask of people, the more permission and support we must give them to get their motivational needs met in healthy ways.

DON'T BE SELFISH

On the way home from work, Kayla felt a strong urge to go biking on her favorite trail. She wasn't sure if Lucas would be interested in joining her since he usually worked later on Tuesdays and was pretty tired after work. She felt guilt creeping in as a voice in her head said, "You should stay home and be with Lucas. You can go biking another day. Don't be selfish."

Kayla loved being on her bike, the wind in her face, and being active in nature. She always felt so good afterward. She messaged Lucas, "If it's okay with you, I'd like to hit the trail tonight after work." No sooner had she pressed "send" when she recognized it. "Damn it! Here I go again, believing that I have to make Lucas happy and that I need his permission to do my thing. That's my Please You Driver. Argh!" She quickly sent another message, "Rewind that. I want to go biking tonight to recharge. I need it to fill my tank. See you later." Kayla still felt a little guilty but also felt a surge of confidence. She started visualizing her bike route as she continued driving home.

Kayla enjoyed biking with Lucas and her friends, but she also liked going alone. She could go where she wanted, stop when she wanted, and take it at her own pace. While she biked, Kayla started musing about her homework, "How do I make sure my elevator is running smoothly?" She reflected on her own Phase motivational need for contact and her Base need for recognition of person and sensory. "Maybe that's why biking is so energizing for me," Kayla wondered. It gave her contact through the movement and physicality of biking. The sights, smells, sounds, and feel of the air definitely fed her senses. But what about her Base need for recognition of person? It seemed to Kayla that this could only happen around other people who loved her and accepted her.

Kayla stopped atop her favorite hill to take in the view and get a drink of water. She couldn't get one phrase out of her head: "Don't be selfish." Even though she knew how energizing and healthy it was for her to go biking, she still felt guilty, like she should be more considerate of her boyfriend's needs. She made a mental note to ask Pauline about it at their next meeting and took off down the hill. Kayla laughed out loud as she imagined herself as a border collie going through an agility course speeding down the hill. "If I'm a dog, how do I show up ready to do my best?"

The answer hit her at the same time that she hit the sharp turn at the bottom of the hill. Braking hard and leaning to her left, Kayla made the turn and skidded to a stop near a small stream. "I gotta eat and I gotta sleep! That's what dogs do." Kayla said to herself, "I can't run the course without food and rest. I'd never take my dog to a competition without proper food and rest. But for years I've been taking myself to work with an empty tank. No wonder I've been miserable." It seemed too obvious to be important, yet it totally made sense.

Kayla was physically tired but emotionally rejuvenated when she got home. Lucas asked if he could come over. Kayla asked him about his day, listened curiously as he shared his opinions about some changes at work, and felt perfectly comfortable focusing on Lucas's agenda and needs for most of the evening. He did ask her once about her day, but Kayla didn't feel compelled to keep the focus on her.

For the next several days Kayla's mind kept going back to her dad. If he was in a Rebel Phase, it made perfect sense why he enjoyed the band with his friends. He got a lot of contact. Yet Kayla struggled with her own feelings of being left out and ignored by him when she was younger. It seemed like he had been selfish spending all that time with his band instead of her. "Maybe Pauline will have a helpful perspective," Kayla decided, and made another mental note.

Pauline surprised Kayla again for their next meeting. Just before heading up to her office, Kayla got a text from Pauline: "I need to head across town to drop something off for my mom. I don't want to cancel our meeting. Wanna come with me and we can talk in the car?" Kayla felt a little bit angry, wondering why Pauline couldn't run her errand later. Why did she need to interrupt their meeting? Kayla also was looking forward to their meeting and didn't want to miss it. She arrived at Pauline's office and said, "I got your text. Sure, I'll come with you. I was looking forward to our meeting."

"I'm sorry to do this, Kayla. My mom lives in a nursing home across town and she is having some medical procedures done later this morning. I have some paperwork they need and I'm trying to get it to the nursing home before they take her to the doctor. I thought about rescheduling, but I was also looking forward to our meeting so that's why I suggested you come along. We'll be in the car for over an hour, so plenty of time to talk. Does this work for you?"

"Sounds good." Kayla felt better, especially since they stopped by the coffee shop before they headed out.

"So what's been on your mind this week, Kayla?" Pauline inquired once they were on their way.

Kayla jumped right in. "Two things don't go together very well, and I'm struggling to reconcile them." Kayla shared her insights about feeding her own motivational needs, and her insight about the dog agility metaphor and not showing up in a good space for so many years. "But there's this nagging voice in my head that keeps saying, 'Don't be selfish.' It's driving me nuts. What's that about?"

Pauline paused for a few seconds before answering. "How did you know? I have been hearing that same voice all morning. When the nursing home called, I knew that running these forms over would interfere with our meeting time. I really value our time, so I struggled with what to do. When I decided to make the run, my inner voice said, 'Why don't you do it later or get someone else to do it. You can't just cancel your meeting with Kayla. Don't be selfish.' Being completely honest, Kayla, the reason I asked you to come along was because I didn't want to look selfish by making my errand more important than our meeting. Pretty lame, huh?"

Kayla was stunned. "You're the boss. You can do whatever you want. My schedule is much more flexible than yours. You don't need to feel guilty."

THE VOICES IN MY HEAD

"Thanks, Kayla. Really, I appreciate that. Let me explain. My Thinker Phase is naturally responsible. I keep my commitments and follow my schedule, sometimes to a fault. When something unexpected comes up, like this morning, I really struggle with it because it throws my schedule off. My Thinker Phase says, 'Keep your schedule. Find a way to make it work. Don't be selfish, don't let Kayla down.' You wouldn't want to be inside my head on days like this!"

"I can relate. So how do you deal with it?" Kayla empathized and was truly curious.

"I remind myself that being self-full is different from being selfish."

"What is self-full?" Kayla asked. "Is that even a word?"

"I don't know, but it's super helpful for me." Pauline explained, "Self-full means taking elegant care of your motivational needs so that you can show up ready to be your best and do your best. It means filling your own tank before you try to deal with others. My Phase is Thinker. My mom is the most important person in my life. I want to be sure she is getting quality care. I'm able to help with logistics and details to make sure that happens. Why wouldn't I make her a priority, especially when there's an urgent situation? It's so obvious. Taking care of her fills my tank. Knowing that I am helping her have the best possible quality of life helps me meet my needs so that I can stay agile with others in my life."

"I totally get that," Kayla empathized again. "Riding my bike is like that for me. It fills my tank. Just the other night I was feeling guilty about going biking by myself without Lucas. But when I got home, I had all this energy to listen to him and meet him where he was at."

"That's the irony, Kayla. We believe that it's noble to put everyone else first, but the reality is that when we meet our own needs first, we energize ourselves to connect more authentically with others."

Kayla made a connection. She energized her best flight attendant voice and recited, "In case there is a loss in cabin pressure, yellow oxygen masks will deploy from the ceiling compartment located above you. Please secure your own mask before assisting others around you."

> When we meet our needs first, we
> energize ourselves to connect more
> authentically with others.

Pauline laughed. "Exactly! That's what I'm talking about. How can you help the people around you when you can't breathe?! I'll admit, I've never actually experienced a loss in cabin pressure so I don't know what I would do if that happened."

"We'd probably all freak out." Kayla pulled down the sun visor, pretending an oxygen mask was falling from the car ceiling, trying to help imaginary people in the back seat while gasping for breath. Pauline and Kayla had a good laugh playing out how absurd this would be.

"In all seriousness, though," Kayla continued once she had recovered from the loss of cabin pressure, "it's a lot easier said than done. People don't always care or appreciate that we need to take care of ourselves. And, what about those voices inside telling us we are being selfish?"

"No kidding, Kayla," Pauline affirmed. "There are also voices outside of us sending these harmful messages. You are probably familiar with the philosophy of servant leadership. I'm all about serving people and being humble, but when we serve others at the expense of our own needs, we aren't helping anyone. There's got to be a balance. There's nothing noble about hurting yourself. That's plain selfish."

"Wait! Did you just say that hurting ourselves is selfish?" Kayla was confused.

NEGLECTING YOUR NEEDS IS SELFISH

"Yes, I did." Pauline explained, "As crazy as it sounds, when we don't take care of ourselves, we are being selfish. It's selfish because we are choosing to soothe our own guilt, avoid conflict, and keep the peace instead of doing the courageous work of setting boundaries and choosing priorities. It's a cop-out."

"That's harsh!" Kayla reacted.

"I'm not attacking people who don't get their needs met," Pauline explained. "I'm saying that it takes a lot of courage and discipline to be self-full. When the world doesn't come to your rescue and voices in your head are telling you to put your needs on the back burner, it takes some serious guts to do the right, healthy thing."

"And as a leader, everyone is looking at you, too," Kayla added.

"Yes. As a leader I am both a role model and a guide. People look to me to see how things are going. They watch how I conduct myself, including how I take care of myself. At ProcessCorp we emphasize that all personality types are okay and that it's okay to take care of yourself in order to show up energized and agile. That means we must also support people taking the necessary steps to do that. The more we ask of people, the more permission and support we must give them to get their motivational needs met in healthy ways."

Kayla reflected on the support she'd received in getting her needs met at ProcessCorp. "I see what you are talking about, Pauline. And I suppose sometimes that means setting boundaries or asking for help."

"Very often that's the case," Pauline agreed. "We are each responsible for getting our needs met, but that doesn't mean we can do it alone. Sometimes we need help. Have you met Mia in IT? She has an Imaginer Base and Phase. Her Phase need is solitude. She thrives on being alone and is perfectly content to work with computers and networks all day long. Too many people interactions wear her out."

"That's crazy! I love being around people. It energizes me." Kayla waited for a response.

WHO IS RESPONSIBLE?

"Yeah. Not for Mia though. It's been a learning process for her to stay healthy. There's a lot of social stuff going on around here, as you know. When Mia first started here, people were always inviting her to hang out, join them on break, or go to happy hour after work.

She went along out of obligation but clearly hated it. One of the biggest breakthroughs for Mia was when she realized that it was okay for her to get solitude at work, and there was nothing wrong with her for wanting to be alone. But she had to own it and take responsibility for it. She was the only one who could educate others about her needs and ask for the kind of support she wanted."

"I bet that was really hard," Kayla empathized.

"It was, and also liberating for Mia," Pauline continued. "Her PCM Profile gave her more confidence and permission, and a language to talk about what was going on. When she started sharing it, people were totally supportive. We all know that it's okay to invite Mia to join us for social stuff. Sometimes she does, sometimes she doesn't. Mia knows it's okay to get solitude when she needs it and we will respect that. It actually works out really well with her job."

"But Mia can't just isolate herself all the time. She's got to be available, right?" Kayla stopped herself from expressing what she really felt, that Mia was being selfish by avoiding people just because she was Imaginer Phase.

"Of course." Pauline was firm. "Mia is responsible for her job duties and for being a team player. She's more than just an Imaginer Phase. She has all six floors in her personality just like you and I. However, getting her Imaginer need for solitude met on a daily basis is the key to her agility. It's the key for her being able to interact with people effectively. You should see when she energizes her Rebel floor. Her humor and wit are like no other!

"It's not like we have to be hooked up to the gas pump all day long, though. Regular fill-ups allow us to travel all over the place. But knowing when, how, and where to fill our tank is still the key to being self-full."

When they arrived at the nursing home, Pauline invited Kayla to come meet her mother and drop off the medical records. Even in the very short time they were there, Kayla could see the strong bond between Pauline and her mother. She could tell how energizing it was for Pauline to help out with important tasks related to her mother's care.

When they got back in the car, Kayla remembered her other question. "I was wondering, is it possible for me to get my Harmonizer recognition of person needs met without other people? I was thinking that I needed others around to love me and accept me."

"Great question, Kayla. Why do you ask?"

"Because I was struggling with going biking alone, yet I felt so good afterward. I get how biking meets my contact and sensory needs, but what about recognition of person?"

"Who's in charge of getting your needs met, Kayla?" Pauline asked.

"Me, I guess." Kayla wasn't sure where this was leading.

Pauline probed further. "Do you ever feel like when you are with others you focus on their needs and aren't as self-full as you want to be, or should be?"

Kayla agreed. "Yeah, quite often. I get energized being with people, especially when I trust them and feel safe with them. But when I'm unsure, I tend to focus more on making sure they are happy, less on my own needs."

"So what about when you go biking by yourself?"

"It's on my terms. Nobody is there so I can focus on me without feeling responsible for someone else's happiness." Kayla immediately reacted to what she heard herself say. "I get it! When I go by myself, I am taking care of me. I am recognizing my own person."

"You got it!" Pauline smiled. "I know a lot of people with Harmonizer Base or Phase who really enjoy taking time for themselves to recharge. It's just like you say, they tune out the rest of the world for a short time so that that they can focus on themselves. It may feel selfish, but it's totally okay and self-full."

"What a relief!" Kayla sighed. "That's so helpful to hear. I don't always need others to recognize me for me. I can do that all by myself, too!"

"Yes. Seeing people through includes ourselves, too," Pauline added. "It's an ongoing process. The better we get at meeting our own needs, the more agile we are with others. When we set appropriate boundaries and ask for help, we allow others to be part of the process and we send the message that it's okay for them to do that, too."

POWERFUL BEYOND MEASURE

Pauline continued, "Nelson Mandela, who led South Africa out of apartheid after 27 years in prison, is famous for saying, 'As we let our own light shine, we unconsciously give other people permission to do the same.' But he was quoting a poem by Marianne Williamson called 'Our Deepest Fear.' It speaks to the importance of owning our own power and helping others do the same.

"In that same poem Williamson starts with, 'Our deepest fear is not that we are inadequate. Our deepest fear is that we are powerful beyond measure. It is our light, not our darkness that most frightens us.' Seeing people through is about getting past those negative voices in our head, letting our light shine, and helping others do the same. If you want to read the whole poem, I'm sure it's on the internet."

When they got back to work, Kayla thanked Pauline for including her on her errand instead of rescheduling and asked, "Any homework this week?"

"Yes. Next time is our last official session for this part of your integration to ProcessCorp and I have an assignment for you. It's more of a project than homework. We call it your PCM Leadership Design. It will require you to reflect on what you've learned and apply it to your life. I'd like to give us two weeks between now and our last session to give you adequate time, so you don't feel rushed. Want to hear about it?"

"I'm intrigued. Yes, I'm ready for my assignment," Kayla responded enthusiastically.

PCM LEADERSHIP DESIGN

Pauline continued, "Your PCM Leadership Design project has four parts." She handed Kayla a worksheet titled My PCM Leadership Design.

"Part One: For each of the six personality types in you, identify another person whom you would consider a role model for that type. In other words, the type might be this person's Base or Phase, and it really shines through. Describe what you've learned to appreciate about that type from them. Then describe the value of this type in you and how it can serve you in a leadership role.

"Part Two: Describe your Phase and Base distress, being specific about observable behaviors that others can see, and that you can recognize. Explain how it impairs you as a leader, and how you will manage it going forward.

"Part Three: Develop a daily action plan for how you positively meet your Phase and Base needs in a healthy way every day. Keep it realistic, things you can actually do every day without compromising your relationships or responsibilities.

"Part Four: Create a personal mission statement that honors your unique personality."

"I get the first parts, but what do you mean by personal mission statement?" Kayla felt like there might be a lot of Persister energy required for this part of the assignment.

Pauline explained, "Most of us are familiar with organizational mission statements focusing on the purpose of the organization, why it exists, and what difference it wants to make in the world. I don't think as leaders we focus enough energy on our own purpose and what difference we want to make in the world. Your PCM personality structure is a wonderful, unique, and powerful thing that gives you the ability to lead in wonderful, unique, and powerful ways. I want you to spend some time reflecting on what might be the purpose of your unique personality. Why are you built this way and what difference could it make in the world? What will you do with it?"

"Do you have a personal mission statement?" Kayla asked.

"Yes, I do. I've updated it a few times."

"Would you be willing to share it with me?"

"Sure, Kayla. Mine goes like this:

My personal mission is to help people execute a plan that maximizes the impact of their unique voice.

"As you know, my Base is Promoter and my Phase is Thinker. This gives me the ability to cut through the chaos and distractions we so often experience, and get to the real issues. I value unique perspectives and I recognize that unless people take personal responsibility around their ideas, they won't make the kind of impact that is most rewarding for themselves and our company. So I use my Promoter Character Strengths to get to the point and focus on actionable strategies. And I use my Thinker Phase to keep focused on responsibility around execution and impact."

"I see what you mean. I also see how your personal mission statement fits with ProcessCorp." Kayla felt a little better since she didn't hear any Persister opinions coming through in Pauline's mission statement.

"Exactly," Pauline agreed. "It works for me, it inspires me, and I believe it captures how I can make the biggest difference using my personality. Kayla, there's no right or wrong personal mission statement. The best answer is the one that fits you best and inspires you to make the most of your personality every day as a leader."

"I think I've got it. See you in two weeks?" Kayla clarified.

"Yes, and it's okay to check in with me if you have any questions between now and then."

Kayla didn't hear the last thing Pauline said because of the negative reactions she had to all the homework. "More writing! All these questions. And a personal mission statement. This is too hard!"

To reenergize herself Kayla decided to go introduce herself to Mia and see if she could find a Rebel connection.

NINE

Seeing People Through

There is no paycheck that can equal the feeling of contentment that comes from being the person you are meant to be.

—Oprah Winfrey

Success is knowing your purpose in life, growing to reach your maximum potential, and sowing seeds that benefit others.

—John Maxwell

Kayla didn't particularly want to work on her PCM Leadership Design project but she forced herself to dabble here and there. She did accept Pauline's invitation to make some time at work for the project. She felt a little weird about it, but nobody seemed to mind. Kayla was conscientious to make sure her teammates knew what she was doing and that it didn't interfere with any other responsibilities. They were all supportive.

Kayla experimented with some of the other suggestions in the personal action plan that was attached to her PCM Profile. She brought in a few pictures from home to put on her desk. She took a risk and wore some of her favorite clothes that were more playful and expressed her creative side. She asked Pauline if there were any new, novel, or creative projects she could work on. Kayla was pleasantly surprised how welcoming her team was of her efforts to meet her Rebel Phase needs, and how good it felt! Her energy and enjoyment for work steadily increased, as did her enthusiasm about her Leadership Design project. She even introduced herself to Mia and had a great conversation but stopped short of inviting her out for coffee. Kayla figured she wouldn't push the social aspect.

When Kayla met with Pauline for their final integration meeting, she felt a mixture of anticipation and sadness. "I'm excited to share my project with you, and sad that our regular time is coming to an end," she disclosed.

"I hear ya, Kayla," Pauline responded. "This is always bittersweet. I really enjoy getting to know new employees and watching them grow. I often wonder if I am getting the better end of the deal! I learn so much every time."

Pauline paused. "Okay, Kayla. Let's get started. This session is all yours. I'm so excited to hear what you came up with."

"Great. Is it okay with you if I start from the top, go in order with the four parts of the project?" Kayla felt a little nervous and found herself losing assertiveness.

"Absolutely, Kayla. There's no right or wrong answers. I am just so happy to learn more about you and how this stuff is impacting your life."

Kayla had her project pulled up on her laptop. "In no particular order, here are my role models of the six types and how they serve me as a leader.

"First is Imaginer. I'm going to have to say my mom. I wouldn't have said that before learning about PCM. I love her and admire her, but never appreciated the value of her Imaginer part before. She worked night shift in the laundry of a big hospital. Most of the time she was alone. I could never do that. I'd go crazy! But she loved it. I think her Imaginer type thrived on that solitude; she could work with her hands instead of interacting with people all day. Even though she was pretty introverted, she found energy to interact with the family when she was at home. I think that's because she got enough solitude at work so she could ride her elevator to her other floors.

She has put up with my dad for almost 30 years! The other thing I admire about her is that she never seemed to get flustered. She was calm no matter what happened.

"I remember when I was eight years old, I fell and cut my head on some playground equipment. I had to go to the ER for a couple of stitches and my mom came to pick me up from school. I was bleeding all over the place and everyone was freaking out except my mom. I remember feeling better when she arrived just because she was so calm.

"How does the Imaginer type in me help me as a leader? It's my least developed floor so I have some work to do. What I have realized is that my Rebel Phase can get pretty excited about stuff and sometimes I don't think before I talk or act. That can get me into trouble. My Imaginer part can help me reflect and ponder things more fully and see other sides to a situation. This could really help me as a leader, being able to see things from different perspectives and imagine other ways of approaching a problem. My sense is that Imaginer types are also nonjudgmental. They take in what comes without a need to evaluate it. People need a nonjudgmental presence in order to feel safe and creative, and my Imaginer can help with that."

"Fabulous insight, Kayla," Pauline reacted. "I certainly value the Imaginer type and had never thought of the part about being a nonjudgmental presence. That's so important when you are trying to foster creativity and innovation. Cool stuff! Pardon the interruption though. Please continue."

"Next is Promoter. My Promoter role model is my dad's best friend and bandmate, Jim. They literally called him the band promoter because it was his job to get gigs. He was really good at making connections and finding opportunities. He was so charming and persuasive, they used to say he could sell ice cubes to Eskimos. Promoters get a bad reputation because of their manipulative distress behavior. I saw that once in a while from Jim, but for the most part, I only saw his amazing charisma. I could watch him perform all night. He had this presence about him that just drew people in. No one was a stranger to him; he could start a conversation with anyone.

"As a leader, I can really see the value of the Promoter when it comes to enthusiasm and optimism. I can use this part of me to help keep things positive and look for opportunities. I can be a champion for the team goals, company mission, or even persuade people to believe in themselves when they are doubting. My Harmonizer and Rebel make for a pretty good cheerleader, but the Promoter adds another level of intensity and action-focus that can come in handy when it's time to seize opportunity or make a bold move. I also realized that the Promoter is brave. Jim used to get even more confident when the stakes were high. I could use some of that when my Harmonizer wants to back away from conflict or avoid a risky situation.

"Any comments about my Promoter choice?" Kayla paused.

"Nope. Lovin' every minute of it! Carry on."

"And now—drum roll—the Rebel!" Kayla was finding her stride. "I was going to pick my dad, but I didn't. I picked a historical figure, Thomas Edison, as my role model. I think he had a strong Rebel part because he was super creative and had a clever outlook on life. My favorite quote of his is, 'I have not failed. I have just found 10,000 ways that will not work.' What a great perspective! This quote has always helped me when I bump up against my Rebel Phase issue of responsibility, especially when I mess up. It reminds me that even during failure we are always learning. That's part of creativity: trying stuff and seeing what works and what doesn't work. It's important that we forgive ourselves, learn from mistakes, and keep trying things.

"I'd say Edison also had a lot of Thinker and Persister energy in his condo because he talked a lot about the value of persistence and hard work.

"Rebel is my Phase so it's probably the most important component of my leadership style. Not only do I need to use that energy positively as a leader, but I must take good care of it because it's the engine that motivates me. My Rebel can be a great asset in leadership because it brings the positive energy and creative problem-solving. We can't be serious and focused all the time! Sometimes we need to lighten up and laugh at ourselves, or explore crazy ideas to see what we come up with. Laughter is the best medicine, you know." Kayla looked at Pauline with a wry smile.

Pauline winked.

"And it's not just fun and games with my Rebel," Kayla continued. "The other thing I bring to leadership is the ability to be in the moment with people. I believe it's called presence. My Rebel type doesn't need to worry about what happened before, or what's going to happen next. I can be fully present in the moment and relish an idea, revel in someone's joy, or commiserate with their discouragement. I think that's another way to support a safe place where people can be themselves and give 100 percent."

Pauline's tone was reflective when she interrupted, "I love that, Kayla. That's something I really struggle with and need to work on. My Thinker is always planning ahead or rehashing the past. I often find myself thinking about what I'm going to say next instead of listening to someone with full attention. Here's a little fun fact. The Rebel hasn't always been named that. One of the earlier names for this type was 'Reveler' precisely because of their ability to enjoy the moment."

"Awesome!" Kayla reacted. "Yeah, I'm a Reveler. One time I cried when I was eating fresh-caught Maine lobster at a seafood restaurant. Lucas thought something was wrong. Nope. I cried because it was so darn good."

Pauline laughed.

"Next is Thinker," Kayla continued. "I chose Mario. I'm really intrigued and impressed with Mario. He is so meticulous and logical with his work. Everything he does fits together and makes sense. He is super knowledgeable and applies what he knows to his work. If he doesn't know something, he learns about it. Me, I would just guess or move on to something else if I didn't know the information. Mario is always early for meetings. He told me once that his philosophy is, 'If you're on time, you're late.' The other thing I admire about Mario is how responsible he is. He takes his duties seriously and always owns up when he makes a mistake. He is constantly looking for ways to learn and grow and improve his contribution. Pretty amazing. Sometimes I worry that he puts too much pressure on himself to be perfect. I suppose it's a fine line between excellence and perfectionism.

"Thinker is the next floor up after my Rebel so I can get there pretty easily. As a leader, this type is helpful for keeping track of information and applying logic to decision-making. When emotions are running high, I can use my Thinker to stay objective and focused on our goals. My Thinker is a very hard worker and loves to complete tasks. Sometimes the difference between good and great is simply the time and effort we put in. When I am supporting Thinker Base or Phase people, I can energize my Thinker to appreciate their need for a logical plan, notice their work, and recognize the value of their time.

"Ready for the last two?" Kayla asked.

"I'm ready!"

"Okay, so the next one is Harmonizer, which is my Base floor. This part has been with me the longest and forms the foundation of my personality. I can certainly see what you said about this part being my preferred way of interacting with the world throughout my life, regardless of changes in my motivational needs.

"My role model is my grandmother. Her name is Josie, and she's turning 90 this year. I love her! My grandma is the most loving, warm, and welcoming person I know. My earliest memories of her include big hugs, sitting on her lap, playing games, and getting the cutest stuffed animals from her for my birthday! Her house always smelled so good, usually because of something she was cooking. She loved hosting guests, so I got to know her neighbors and friends really well. I always felt safe and valuable with grandma Josie. Even when I did something wrong, she had a way of disciplining me that let me know she was angry about my behavior, but she still loved me unconditionally. Did I mention she was the best hugger ever?"

Pauline smiled, "Hugs are the best. For Harmonizers, at least!"

Kayla continued, "Harmonizer energy supports a safe and welcoming environment that values each person for who they are. Even though we don't all want hugs, my Harmonizer can totally get behind the philosophy that different people need different things to function at their best. The Platinum Rule was a big eye-opener for me. My Harmonizer cares about people and the Platinum Rule gives me a better way to show that caring in a way that's not self-centered. I'm good at tuning into how others are feeling. I just have a sense about it. My friends tell me I have 'feel-o-meters' that can pick up how people are doing even without them saying anything. This can come in handy as a leader to help me stay tuned in to *how* people are doing, not just *what* they are doing.

"Any comments before I do Persister?" Kayla paused.

"Nope, I'm ready to hear it." Pauline was sitting on the edge of her chair.

"My Persister role model is Lucas's dad. I was going to pick Lucas, but we've talked enough about him," Kayla chuckled. "His dad is a stellar example of the Persister type. He started his construction company from the ground up with a clear vision that is never compromised. Treat your people with respect, set high standards, and exceed customer expectations. He walks the talk. He's a tough boss and expects a lot from his people, but he also treats them with respect. He started a mentoring program for men who have struggled to maintain employment or have been in jail. He gives them a chance to work for him and requires that they meet personally with him once a week. He listens to their stories and offers guidance, like a father. This program has been a huge success and he's even gotten recognition from the mayor for it. Lucas really looks up to his dad.

"I've been thinking about the Persister type in me and I came up with this analogy. My Persister part is like my backbone. It's what keeps me upright and standing tall. It is the part of me that maintains a posture of integrity and purpose. As a leader, I can use my Persister to keep us focused on what matters most. It's the part that reminds me to say what I mean and do what I say. It can give me courage to speak my truth and share my opinion about what's right and wrong, even when it might not be popular. I bet a lot of our client companies have leaders with strong Persister parts in them. They are looking for consistency, dependability, trustworthiness, and integrity. My Persister can stay tuned into that and make sure we bring that character to all of our relationships."

"You nailed it, Kayla!" Pauline affirmed. "I've experienced the same thing. I've noticed in positions of higher scope and authority, particularly in more traditional companies, there's a lot more Per-sister energy. In newer companies I am seeing more Rebel and Har-monizer energy because they recognize how important safety, inclusion, and creativity are to success."

"So here comes the not so pretty stuff, part two about distress," Kayla said, half joking. "I'll start with my Base Harmonizer distress since it's been with me the longest. When I don't get my Base moti-vational needs met in positive ways, my first sign of distress is that I get tentative and play it safe. I worry about making people upset so I don't ask directly for what I want. It's really sneaky. Most often I start a sentence with, 'Is it okay if . . .' or 'Maybe we could . . .' in-stead of just saying it. This is a problem in leadership because it shows lack of confidence. Not that we need to be confident all the time, but it's important that leaders are comfortable with who they are and are willing to speak their mind.

"My deeper Harmonizer distress was more common before I Phased to Rebel. I would start to second-guess myself, wondering if I'm really worthwhile and if I deserve to be here. I would criticize myself with statements like, 'That was stupid!' or 'They don't care what you have to say.' Eventually it influenced my behavior, and I would say silly things, like, 'This is probably a dumb idea, but what if we went out to eat tonight?' Like, really!? It's just a setup for rejec-tion. I made silly mistakes, not because I was dumb, but because I was questioning myself. Then, when people reacted negatively, I would take it as confirmation that I really was dumb or worthless.

"It's pretty obvious how this could harm my credibility and ef-fectiveness as a leader. Nobody wants a leader who puts themselves down and invites everyone to either criticize them or feel sorry for them. I've worked for leaders like this and it's really awkward.

"So how do I manage this? The first part is becoming aware of the signs. PCM has really helped me recognize stuff going on inside of me that I never realized was distress and negative attention. Since my Phase shifted to Rebel, probably when I went to college, I haven't experienced the deeper Harmonizer distress very often at all. That's probably because I deal with anger more effectively now. I don't let stuff build up inside and I'm more willing to say something when

I'm angry. What I can improve is giving myself permission to take care of me, even if that means doing things alone, like riding my bike or curling up with a good book. I'm glad Lucas supports me spending my time outside of work with some of my new work friends. This really fills my tank. Something else I've been surprised about here at ProcessCorp is how open people are about their feelings, positive and negative. I love to talk about feelings and feel connected in that way."

"I'm so glad you can get your Harmonizer needs met at work as well, Kayla," Pauline affirmed. "I feel happy hearing that. What about your Rebel Phase?"

Kayla was ready for that question, "My Rebel Phase is a bit newer to me, so I'm still getting the hang of it. We've talked quite a bit about my Rebel distress in our sessions. At first, I feel confused, like I don't know what's going on. I try hard to understand but I don't ask for help or get clarification. If I don't recognize that, I can quickly slip into blamer mode to get negative attention. I get really negative about everyone and want to make it everyone else's problem. I can get whiny, which drives Lucas crazy. Even worse, I sometimes say, 'I don't care!' when someone is trying to get me to take things seriously. It's not that I don't care, it's that I don't want to feel responsible; that's my Rebel Phase issue. So I act like I don't care and it really pushes people's buttons. All it does is invite more negative attention from people. Provoking is definitely my negative intention!

"Here at ProcessCorp I've learned so much about how to get my Rebel Phase need for contact met positively. I move around a lot and love making contact with different people throughout the day. The social stuff is great. I'm enjoying biking more than ever, even when I do it alone. Last week I asked you for something extra novel or creative I could work on. That's an example of me taking initiative to do things that help get my needs met. I'd like to get back into playing my guitar. My dad tried to teach me when I was growing up, but I never really practiced. It was boring. I'm going to look into lessons. That could be really fun!

"Like I said, my Rebel Phase is a work in progress, so I'm learning every day. Oh, and the most important thing: When I bump up against my Phase issue of Responsibility, I repeat the mantra, 'Feel it, share it, ask for help, solve it with your special set of skills.'"

"Wonderful!" Pauline exclaimed. "We are all here to support you! You are a rock star!"

Kayla continued with Part Three of her Leadership Design project. "The more I do the stuff I just mentioned, the better off I'll be. For my daily action plan, I put together a few things I can build into my routine to help me stay healthy. These are things over which I have control, so I don't have to rely on others to make the first move.

1. I need my sleep. I feel so much better when I get enough sleep and don't have to rush in the mornings. For the most part I can control how much sleep I get.
2. Quality time with friends. I want to do more things with my friends who accept me the way I am and like to have fun.
3. Biking. If I feel like biking alone, I will give myself permission to do that. If I want company, I will ask someone.
4. At work, I will make a point each day to reach out to different personality types around me and practice seeing them through with the PCM skills I am learning. If I'm not sure how, I will ask them for suggestions."

"What a wonderful plan, Kayla," Pauline spoke up. "I really like how you focused on things you can control. Much of life is out of our control, so the more we focus on keeping our tank filled, the more resilient we will be when life throws us curves. I encourage you to keep this plan front and center and make adjustments as you go. I am sure you will find some things don't work as well as you anticipated, and you'll discover other things that work great."

"Thanks for the encouragement. I will." Kayla felt empowered. "Now for the final part, the personal mission statement. This was the hardest, but I came up with something. I kept trying to create this perfect masterpiece, but I remembered you saying that you've modified yours several times. That helped take the pressure off for me.

"My personal mission statement is:

"My mission is to help people realize their full value so they can make a positive ruckus, and have fun doing it!"

Kayla held her breath.

Pauline closed her eyes and paused as she let Kayla's mission statement sink in. Then she erupted, "You are a trip, Kayla! I love it! What a great expression of who you are and how that can make the world a better place! You took some risk putting yourself out there like that. Good for you!"

Kayla felt an inner peace and joy come over her. She had taken a risk and it felt so good. For a week she had stressed over using the word *ruckus* but kept coming back to it. She had first learned the word while reading one of her favorite marketing blogs by Seth Godin, who was always encouraging people to go make a ruckus— in a good way, of course. Kayla wondered how much Rebel energy Seth had in his condo. Regardless, it gave her permission to let her light shine, and she was proud of herself for putting it into her personal mission statement.

"I'm glad you like it," Kayla began. "But I didn't write it for you. I wrote it for me. I like it." They both laughed. Kayla reveled.

After a few moments, Pauline spoke. "Everyone at ProcessCorp has their own PCM Leadership Design. I want you to keep this where you can look at it regularly. It will become an integral part of your personal and professional development plan. It's okay to update it as you gain more awareness and confidence in the skills of PCM. This is part of our culture so you can count on PCM being around you every day. The more you practice and develop your skills, the more effective you will be as a leader.

"Kayla, you've made so much progress and it's been a joy going through this with you. You really are a remarkable person and I'm glad you are part of the ProcessCorp family."

Kayla felt the tears welling up. She didn't hold back though. Hers were tears of joy, purpose, and anticipation. She couldn't help herself. "Pauline, can I give you a hug? I am so grateful for our time together and all that I've learned."

"Absolutely, Kayla!"

Appendix

CREATING YOUR PCM LEADERSHIP DESIGN

Use this guide to develop your own Process Communication Model Leadership Design. For the most accurate assessment of your own personality structure, go to SeeingPeopleThrough.com to obtain a personalized PCM Key to Leadership Profile. Use the information from your profile to assist you in filling out the worksheet below. If you don't have a PCM Profile, use the Resource Guides in each chapter to make your best guess as to your personality structure and current Phase. A downloadable version of this worksheet is available at SeeingPeopleThrough.com.

Would you prefer to work through this with the help of a PCM Certified Professional? Find one near you by visiting SeeingPeople Through.com.

MY PCM PERSONALITY STRUCTURE

Use the table below to indicate the order of the six Kahler personality types in your personality condo, starting with the Base at the bottom, moving up in decreasing order of importance and energy for you. Indicate how much energy you have in each floor (0–100 percent). Below the table, indicate your current Phase floor and corresponding Phase motivational needs. Consider Tables 1, 2, and 6 as guides.

Personality Type in Me	My Energy in This Floor

My current Phase floor is: _____.

My Phase motivational needs are: _____.

PART 1: MY PERSONALITY ROLE MODELS

In this table write in the six personality types in you, in the same order as your personality structure. For each personality type in you, identify a role model in your life who epitomizes the positive qualities of that type. Describe what you've learned to appreciate about that type from this role model, and how it serves you in leadership. Consider Tables 1, 2, and 6 as guides.

Personality Type in Me	My Role Model	What I Appreciate about This Type	How It Serves Me in Leadership

PART 2: MANAGING MY DISTRESS

In the tables below, identify your Phase and Base distress, being specific about observable behaviors that others can see, and you can recognize. Explain how it impairs you as a leader, and how you will manage it going forward. Consider using Tables 5, 7, 8, 9, 11, and 12 as guides.

My Phase is: _____.

My Phase Distress Behaviors	How My Phase Distress Impairs Me as a Leader	How I Will Manage My Phase Distress

My Base is: _____.
If Base and Phase are the same, skip this section.

My Base Distress Behaviors	How My Base Distress Impairs Me as a Leader	How I Will Manage My Base Distress

PART 3: MY DAILY ACTION PLAN FOR BEING SELF-FULL

Describe how you will positively meet your Phase and Base needs in a healthy way every day. Keep it realistic, including things you can actually do every day without compromising your relationships or responsibilities. Where appropriate, indicate who you will ask for help.

My Phase is:_____

My Phase Motivational Needs are:_____

How I Will Meet My Needs	Who I Will Ask for Help

My Base is:_____

My Base Motivational Needs are:_____

If Base and Phase are the same, skip this section.

How I Will Meet My Needs	Who I Will Ask for Help

PART 4: MY PERSONAL MISSION STATEMENT

Create a personal mission statement that leverages your unique personality to make a difference in the world.

My Personal Mission Statement

_____

_____

_____

_____

Notes

Introduction

1   When I began using PCM in therapy, my treatment outcomes improved dramatically. So much so that Blue Cross Blue Shield, one of the major insurance providers in Kansas, placed me on a select list of clinicians who did not need preapproval for payment. This was because my patients' outcomes were in the top 10 percent statewide. I attribute this to how PCM helped me connect better with patients, more quickly get to the real issues, and offer more effective mechanisms for self-care and recovery. A great side effect was that it helped depathologize and normalize a lot of what people were experiencing.

2   WD40 is the brand name of a common household lubricant sold in the United States. The name has become synonymous with getting things unstuck and helping lubricate for smoother operation.

3   "Store," Kahler Communications, https://www.kahlercommunications.com/store.html.

4   Ryan Donlan, Eric Hampton, and Nate Regier, "Effects of Process Communication Model (PCM) Training," *Training Magazine*, November–December 2017, https://trainingmag.com/trgmag-article/effects-process-communication-model-pcm-training/.

Chapter 2

1   "Taibi Kahler," Exaudian Consulting, http://exaudian.com/taibi-kahler/.

Chapter 4

1   Gallup, "State of the American Manager: Analytics and Advice for Leaders," 2015.

2   Interaction safety is a central theme in Frederick A. Miller and Judith Katz, *Safe Enough to Soar: Accelerating Trust, Inclusion & Collaboration in the Workplace* (Oakland, CA: Berrett-Koehler, 2015).

3   This fictional example is based on real results from Wesley Medical Center, a 2,500-employee HCA hospital. Next Element delivered PCM training and support for nurse managers to address problems with turnover. In one year, they reduced turnover by 2.5 percent, saving $250,000 for a 500 percent return on investment.

4   John Izzo, *The Purpose Revolution: How Leaders Create Engagement and Competitive Advantage in an Age of Social Good* (Oakland, CA: Berrett-Koehler, 2018). Dan Pink, *Drive: The Surprising Truth about What Motivates Us* (New York: Riverhead Books, 2009).

5   MUSE School CA, www.museschool.org.

Chapter 5

1   Compassion is the practice of demonstrating that people are valuable, capable, and responsible: the three switches of The Compassion Mindset. Learn more at https://thecompassionmindset.com/.

2   The Irony of Intent was originally conceptualized and developed by Nate Regier and Taibi Kahler, and further refined with help from Robert Wert.

3   Arbinger Institute, *Leadership and Self-Deception: Getting Out of the Box* (Oakland, CA: Berrett-Koehler, 2010).

Chapter 6

1   Patrick Lencioni, *The Five Dysfunctions of a Team: A Leadership Fable* (San Francisco, CA: Jossey-Bass, 2002).

Acknowledgments

So many people and experiences have shaped this book. Taibi Kahler, your brilliant mind discovered and mapped a model of human personality and behavior unlike anything we've seen. Your big heart guided you to build out a model that enhanced relationships and self-care. Your imagination saw the complexity and nuance of personality and created a system for easy navigation.

My team at Next Element, thank you for your eternal curiosity and playful spirit. PCM is truly like an archeological dig, and you show up on site every day ready to explore what's next.

Among the worldwide network of PCM Trainers, Master Trainers, and Certifying Master Trainers, there is a very special community whose curiosity and commitment to living this model goes beyond just teaching it. The ideas in this book have been honed through many late-night conversations and enthusiastic gatherings around the world. Thank you for your support and engagement.

John Simmering, thank you for introducing me to PCM and for believing in me to be a worthy steward of this gift. It has changed my life for the better.

Thank you to Cyril Collignon, President of Kahler Communications, for your leadership and vision to bring PCM to every corner of the world.

Thousands of people have contributed to this journey as clients of Next Element, making the commitment to receive training or coaching, and taking the risk to become more and do more with PCM. Our mission with PCM has been to live it, make it accessible, and help manifest its potential. Our clients' skepticism and questions, resistance, and successes have been the friction that honed our craft. Thank you.

My first job out of graduate school was as a clinical psychologist working for a regional behavioral health hospital. I was a jack-of-all-trades at first, doing inpatient addictions groups, outpatient therapy, group therapy, and neuropsychological testing. Everything changed, though, when I participated in my first ropes course experience. The hospital had a beautiful adventure ropes course and used it to enhance many of their other services, as well as corporate team-building with outside groups. I'd never heard of using adventure-based challenge elements to facilitate personal and team development. I was immediately hooked.

This is where I met Jamie Remsberg. Jamie was the director of the adventure ropes course. She designed it, built it, trained and mentored all the facilitators, and developed the programming. Before I was introduced to the Process Communication Model® and before I met Dr. Taibi Kahler, the originator of PCM, Jamie showed me what it meant to see people through. She is the most gifted facilitator I've ever met, with an uncanny ability to be present, bring out the best in people, and facilitate personal responsibility with a soft touch. She epitomizes the balance between self-care and attention to others. She lives her life with remarkable intention and focus on relationships. As she's moved into training, coaching, and mentoring, these skills and qualities of character continue to be a priceless gift for her clients and for our team at Next Element.

That was 20 years ago. Since then, Jamie and I became work colleagues, friends, and cofounders of Next Element. Over these many years of growing and learning together, Jamie hasn't been the most vocal and she's never sought the limelight. She doesn't need the credit, humbly seeking only to make a positive difference and live the tools she teaches. In my view, Jamie's biggest contribution to this book is her unwavering and deep commitment to seeing people through. She has taught me and so many others what it means and helped us stay true to this guiding principle.

Index

About the Author

Nate Regier, PhD, is a founding owner and the CEO of Next Element, a global leadership training firm dedicated to bringing more compassion to every workplace. He is an international speaker, trainer, coach, and advisor. Nate is a Process Communication Model Certifying Master Trainer and Next Element is a PCM distributor for the United States.

Nate is a guest on multiple podcasts and writes for many publications, including *Chief Learning Officer*, *Training Magazine*, *Fast Company*, HR.com, *Forbes*, and Association for Talent Development (ATD). He has published two other books: *Beyond Drama: Transcending Energy Vampires*, and *Conflict Without Casualties: A Field Guide for Leading with Compassionate Accountability*. Nate is codeveloper of Next Element's Leading Out of Drama® and The Compassion Mindset® training and coaching systems.

Nate was born and currently lives in Kansas. He grew up in Zaire and Botswana as the son of missionary parents during the 1970s and '80s. Before founding Next Element, he spent 11 years working as a clinical psychologist after completing his doctorate at the University of Kansas.

Nate is married to Julie and has three daughters. Their family enjoys cooking together and spending time at the lake or in the mountains whenever possible. He is an avid BBQer, and competes with his team, who call themselves Three Men and a Butt. Check it out at threemenandabutt.com.

Nate would love to connect with you:

Website: SeeingPeopleThrough.com
LinkedIn: NateRegier
Facebook: Next Element
Twitter: @NextNate
Instagram: nate_regier
Mobile: 316–772–6174

Take the Next Step

Developing your leadership skills requires intentional effort and support. Here are some ways you can continue your journey using PCM to unleash your leadership potential.

1. Invite your peers, supervisor, and employees to take the PCM Profile so you can become aware of their personality structure and work on how to best communicate with each person on your team.
2. Download and use the free discussion guide for your own learning, in a team discussion, or in a class you are teaching.
3. Bring PCM training to your organization. Find a PCM certified professional near you.
4. Engage a PCM certified coach to guide you in realizing your leadership goals.

You will benefit personally and professionally from any investment you make in PCM. Your life, your organization, and your relationships will be better because of your efforts.

Take the next step by visiting SeeingPeopleThrough.com.

Also by Nate Regier

Conflict without Casualties
A Field Guide for Leading with Compassionate Accountability

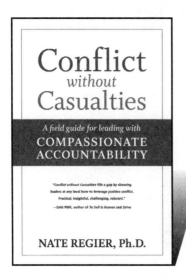

Clinical psychologist Dr. Nate Regier believes that most organizations are terrified of conflict. But conflict isn't the problem. According to Regier, it's all about how we use the energy. When people misuse conflict energy, it becomes drama: they struggle against themselves or each other to feel justified about their negative behavior. The cost to companies, teams, and relationships is staggering. The alternative, says Regier, is compassionate accountability: struggling with others through conflict. Discover the Compassion Cycle, an elegant model for balancing empathy, care, and transparency with boundaries, goals, and standards. Provocative, illuminating, and highly practical, this book helps us avoid the casualties of conflict through openness, resourcefulness, and persistence.

Paperback, ISBN 978-1-5230-8260-5
PDF ebook, ISBN 978-1-5230-8261-2
ePub ebook, ISBN 978-1-5230-8262-9
Digital audio, ISBN 978-1-5230-8264-3

Berrett–Koehler Publishers, Inc.
www.bkconnection.com   **800.929.2929**

✦ Berrett–Koehler
BK Publishers

Berrett-Koehler is an independent publisher dedicated to an ambitious mission: *Connecting people and ideas to create a world that works for all.*

Our publications span many formats, including print, digital, audio, and video. We also offer online resources, training, and gatherings. And we will continue expanding our products and services to advance our mission.

We believe that the solutions to the world's problems will come from all of us, working at all levels: in our society, in our organizations, and in our own lives. Our publications and resources offer pathways to creating a more just, equitable, and sustainable society. They help people make their organizations more humane, democratic, diverse, and effective (and we don't think there's any contradiction there). And they guide people in creating positive change in their own lives and aligning their personal practices with their aspirations for a better world.

And we strive to practice what we preach through what we call "The BK Way." At the core of this approach is *stewardship*, a deep sense of responsibility to administer the company for the benefit of all of our stakeholder groups, including authors, customers, employees, investors, service providers, sales partners, and the communities and environment around us. Everything we do is built around stewardship and our other core values of *quality, partnership, inclusion, and sustainability.*

This is why Berrett-Koehler is the first book publishing company to be both a B Corporation (a rigorous certification) and a benefit corporation (a for-profit legal status), which together require us to adhere to the highest standards for corporate, social, and environmental performance. And it is why we have instituted many pioneering practices (which you can learn about at www.bkconnection.com), including the Berrett-Koehler Constitution, the Bill of Rights and Responsibilities for BK Authors, and our unique Author Days.

We are grateful to our readers, authors, and other friends who are supporting our mission. We ask you to share with us (at www.bkconnection.com/impact) examples of how BK publications and resources are making a difference in your lives, organizations, and communities.

Dear reader,

Thank you for picking up this book and welcome to the worldwide BK community! You're joining a special group of people who have come together to create positive change in their lives, organizations, and communities.

What's BK all about?

Our mission is to connect people and ideas to create a world that works for all.

Why? Our communities, organizations, and lives get bogged down by old paradigms of self-interest, exclusion, hierarchy, and privilege. But we believe that can change. That's why we seek the leading experts on these challenges—and share their actionable ideas with you.

A welcome gift.

To help you get started, we'd like to offer you a **free copy** of one of our bestselling ebooks:

www.bkconnection.com/welcome

When you claim your **free ebook**, you'll also be subscribed to our blog.

Our freshest insights.

Access the best new tools and ideas for leaders at all levels on our blog at ideas.bkconnection.com.

Sincerely,

Your friends at Berrett-Koehler

Certified

Corporation